Unreal Engine 4

for Beginners

David Nixon

Unreal Engine 4 for Beginners

ISBN 0-692-84198-9
ISBN 978-0-692-84198-3

CONTENTS

CHAPTER 1 – GETTING STARTED

CHAPTER 2 – BASIC CONCEPTS

CHAPTER 3 – THE LEVEL EDITOR

CHAPTER 4 – ACTORS

CHAPTER 5 – BLUEPRINTS

CHAPTER 6 – PLAYERS & INPUT

CHAPTER 7 – COLLISIONS

CHAPTER 8 – USER INTERFACES

CHAPTER 9 – AUDIO

CHAPTER 10 – ADDITIONAL TOPICS

1

Getting Started

1.1 Licensing

In this book, you will be learning how to use what many consider to be the best game engine in the industry. The Unreal Engine has been used to create several blockbuster games and game franchises, including BioShock, Gears of Wars, Splinter Cell, Rainbow 6, Borderlands, Dishonored, Mass Effect, and many more.

The biggest disadvantage of the Unreal Engine was that, for most of its existence, it was too expensive for anyone but large companies and wealthy individuals. Epic Games, the creators of the Unreal Engine, realized that because of this, there were huge numbers of budding game developers starting their game development lives getting used to competing engines. These other engines were being offered for free, in exchange for a percentage of any profits made from the games.

Due to this increasing competition, Epic Games decided to adopt a similar business model. In March 2015, the Unreal Engine became completely free to download and use. The only stipulation is that if you create something on it that makes more than $3000 in a single quarter (meaning a quarter of a year), then you have to pay a 5% royalty to Epic Games for any sales above the $3000.

Now, for the first time ever, the Unreal Engine is accessible to amateurs, hobbyists and indie developers, and not just the major game studios of the world.

1.2 Registration

You will need to register an account with Epic Games, the creators of the Unreal Engine, in order to download and install it. To register an account, perform the following steps:

1. Open a web browser and go to unrealengine.com.

2. Look for a blue button that says "Get Unreal" and click on it. You should now be taken to a screen where you can register for an account with Epic Games.

Figure 1.2.1 – The form to register an account with Epic Games

3. Enter your First and Last name.

4. Choose a display name. This will be used if you post on the Epic Games forums.

5. Enter an email address. Choose a password to use that is at least 7 characters and contains at least 1 number and 1 letter.

6. Once you have read and agree to the Terms of Service, click on the checkbox indicating you have done so.

7. Click on the large button that says "Sign Up."

8. You will be given an End User License Agreement to read. Once you have read and agree to it, check the checkbox indicating you have done so, then click on the "Accept" button.

1.3 Download & Installation

After completing registration, you will be taken to a screen where you can download the installer for something called the *Epic Games Launcher*. Perform the following steps:

1. Click on the large "Download" button to begin the download.

2. Once the download has finished, open the file that was downloaded. The filename should start with "EpicGamesLauncherInstaller" and the file extension will be *.msi*. Choose a folder path where you want to install the launcher and then click on the "Install" button.

3. Once it finishes installing, it should open automatically. If it doesn't, look for an Epic Games Launcher shortcut on your desktop and double-click on that. It will ask you for the email and password you provided during registration. Enter that information and click "Sign In."

4. Now you will be on the home screen of the Epic Games Launcher. From here, click on the "Unreal Engine" tab. In that tab, click on the yellow button that says "Install Engine."

Figure 1.3.1 – The Install Engine button

5. You will be given another End User License Agreement to read and if you agree with it, click in the checkbox, then click "Accept." The Launcher will now begin to download the latest version of the Engine. Once the download completes, the Launcher will automatically install it.

6. Once the installation is complete, the yellow button will now say "Launch," and if you click on it, that will launch the Engine.

1.4 Chapter 1 Quiz

1. What is the name of the company that created and owns the Unreal Engine?

2. If you make $2500 in a single quarter from a game you developed using the Unreal Engine, how much of a royalty fee do you owe for that quarter?

3. If you make $4000 in a single quarter from a game you developed using the Unreal Engine, how much of a royalty fee do you owe for that quarter?

4. True or False: You must register an account in order to download and install the Unreal Engine.

5. What is the name of the application that launches the Unreal Engine?

Answers

1. Epic Games

2. $0. You only owe a royalty on sales above $3000 for a quarter.

3. $50. You must pay a 5% royalty on sales above $3000 for a quarter. 4000 - 3000 = 1000 * .05 = 50

4. True

5. Epic Games Launcher

2

Basic Concepts

2.1 Projects

In the context of the Unreal Engine, a *project* is the unit that stores all the information for an individual game. Meaning each game you create will be stored in its own project.

For example, for a first-person shooter game, you might have a project called "ShooterProject." If you wanted to work on another game, a puzzle game, you would create a new project and perhaps call it "PuzzleProject." So if you are working on five different games, you should have five different projects, one for each game.

Unreal Project Browser

To launch the Unreal Project Browser:

1. Go to your desktop and double-click on the Epic Games Launcher shortcut that you created during installation.

2. Click the yellow "Launch" button in the upper-left corner.

The *Unreal Project Browser* is where you can open your existing projects or create new ones. It is divided into two tabs.

Projects Tab

The first tab is simply called *Projects* and will be selected by default whenever the Project Browser first opens. This tab is for existing projects. It contains thumbnail images of all existing projects that the Project Browser was able to find, which would include any projects within the installation directory, and any projects you previously created or opened using this installation of Unreal.

Figure 2.1.1 – The Projects tab of the Unreal Project Browser

To open a project, simply double-click on it, or select it and click the "Open" button in the bottom-right corner, and it will open the Unreal Editor and load that project into it.

If you have lots of projects and need help finding one, you can enter all or part of the name of the project in the search bar at the top and it will narrow down the results based on what you entered.

As previously mentioned, the Projects tab will only list the projects that the Project Browser could find. For example, if you were to download an existing project from the Internet onto your desktop, then the Project Browser won't know about it until you open that project. This is what the "Browse" button in the bottom-right corner is for. In this situation, you would need to click the Browse button and browse to that project file on your desktop and open it from there. Once you open it, from then on, the Project Browser will know about it and it will appear in the list.

In the upper-right corner of the Project Browser there are two buttons – *Refresh* and *Marketplace*. The Refresh button is used to refresh the list of project thumbnails. Again, let's say that you download a project from the Internet, but instead of saving it to the desktop, you saved it in the installation directory instead. In that scenario, the Project Browser will be able to find it. However, it won't appear in the list until you click the Refresh button.

If you click the Marketplace button, this will take you to the Marketplace tab of the Epic Games Launcher where you can download existing environments, objects, characters, etc. either for free or for a price.

In the bottom-left corner is a checkbox labeled "Always load last project on startup." If you check this, the next time you hit the Launch button in the Games Launcher, it will skip the Project Browser altogether and automatically open the last project you worked on. This is useful if you plan to be working on only one project for several days, weeks, or months at a time. It will allow you to skip this step every time.

If you do this and then want to open a new or different project, you can still do that through the File menu of the Unreal Editor. If you later decide you *do* want the Project Browser to open on launch, you can change this setting in the Editor Preferences.

New Project Tab

The second tab is the *New Project* tab. This tab has two tabs itself – a *Blueprint* tab and a *C++* tab. On the Blueprint tab, there are twelve options to choose from – a blank project, and eleven template projects.

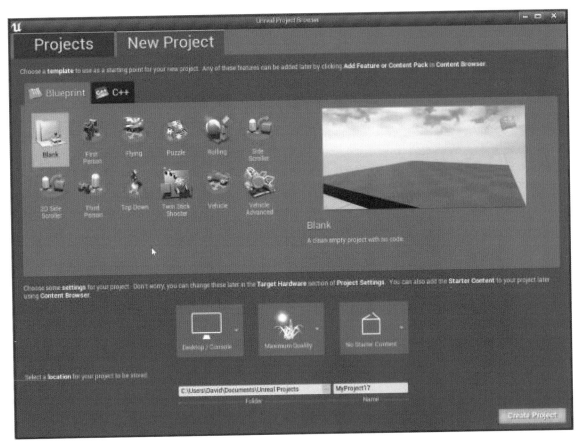

Figure 2.1.2 – The New Project tab of the Unreal Project Browser

The templates are all based around common game types. For example, the *First Person* template will load with several features common to first-person games already hooked up and ready to go. For a racing game, the *Vehicle* template would make a good choice. If you don't choose these features here, you still have the option to add them in later if you want. You could choose a blank project to start with and then add in "First Person" features later, within the Editor.

Towards the bottom of the tab, there are three different settings available to configure. You also have the option to change any of these settings later within the Editor.

Figure 2.1.3 – Settings available on the New Project tab

First, you can choose the overall class of hardware that you are planning to develop your game for. You can choose between *Desktop/Console* for developing computer and console games and *Mobile/Tablet* for developing phone and tablet games.

Next, you have the option of choosing between *Maximum Quality* and *Scalable 3D or 2D*. In general, you would pair the Desktop/Console setting with Maximum Quality, and Mobile/Tablet with Scalable 3D or 2D, which makes this setting somewhat redundant. However, if you wanted to, for example, create a desktop game that could operate using minimal resources, you could pair the "Desktop" and "Scalable" settings together.

Lastly, you have the option of choosing between *With Starter Content* and *No Starter Content*. Choosing the blank template will start you off with no code, but if you wanted to start with a truly empty project you would choose the blank template along with the No Starter Content setting. However, the With Starter Content setting is useful as it will load into your project, from the start, a lot of basic content you can use to get you going such as materials, basic shapes, etc.

Finally, when you have selected the template you want to use and have chosen your settings, you just need go to the bottom of the window and choose where you want the project to be saved, give it a name, and click the *Create Project* button in the bottom-right. This will open the Unreal Editor and load a new project into it based on the settings you chose.

2.2 Levels

A *Level*, in the context of the Unreal Engine, can be defined as a collection of objects and their properties that together define an area of gameplay.

That's the technical definition, but an easy way to visualize this is, if you've ever played a fighting game such as Super Smash Bros, or SoulCalibur, or Mortal Kombat, you know that each match takes place in a different location. The first match might take place in a palace and the next one in a forest, and so on. Each of these different locations would be its own Level within the Unreal Editor.

Also, think of FPS games such as Call of Duty or Battlefield. When you're playing multiplayer, you might get asked to choose a map for the match to take place in. Each of those maps are their own Level.

Levels are loaded and unloaded into memory one-at-a-time. So if you're playing a game where you're in a town, and you can walk around the town and every time you enter or exit one of the buildings in the town, the game has to load; then that means that the outside of the town is a single Level, and each building interior is its own Level.

A single game may consist of only one Level, but often will consist of many Levels. Major releases often contain hundreds of Levels.

Creating, Opening & Saving Levels

To create a new Level, go to File > New Level, or use the shortcut *Ctrl+N*.

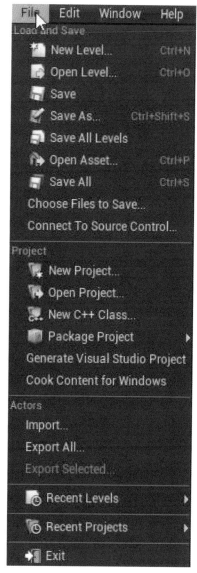

Figure 2.2.1 – The File Menu

You have the option of choosing between "Default" and "Empty Level." "Default" will start you off with some basic stuff already added, including a platform, an atmosphere, some lighting, etc. The "Empty Level" option will start you off with a completely empty Level.

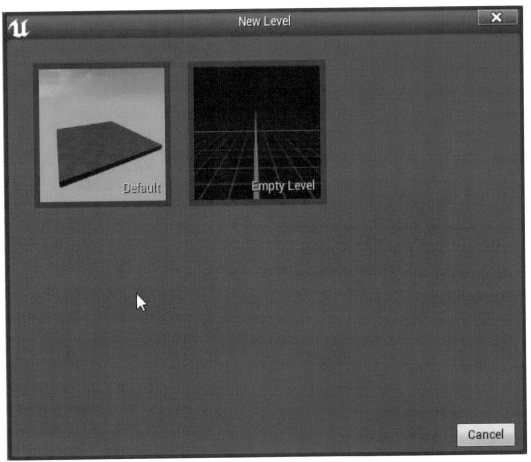

Figure 2.2.2 – You can choose between Default and Empty Level when creating a new Level

To open an already existing Level, go to File > Open Level, or use the shortcut *Ctrl+O*. From there, navigate through the Content folder to find the Level you want, then double-click to open it.

There are multiple options available for saving. You can go to File > Save to save it with its current name. Or you can select "Save As," and save it under a different name. If you have multiple Levels that are unsaved, and want to save them all, you can select "Save All Levels."

In addition to Levels, it is possible to open and save other Assets as well. An *Asset* is anything that can be used to help develop your game that can be saved and opened. For example, anything you can open or add to your game within the Content Browser is an Asset.

If you want to open an existing Asset for editing, you would select "Open Asset," or use *Ctrl+P*, and then select the Asset you want to open from the list.

To save everything you have open, including all Levels and other Assets, select "Save All," or simply press *Ctrl+S*. To save only some of the files you have open, select "Choose Files to Save..." and select which of the unsaved files you want to save.

Finally, if you want to open a Level that you worked on recently, it may be quicker to go down to "Recent Levels" and select the Level from that list, rather than using the "Open Level" dialog.

Playing a Level

You can test your Levels directly in the Editor by clicking on the Play button at the top of the screen. This will simulate the Level immediately, without having to do a full build of the game, so you can quickly test things as you develop them.

Figure 2.2.3 – The Play Button

To view the Level fullscreen, or to exit fullscreen, press the *F11* key. To stop the simulation, press the Stop button at the top of the screen.

2.3 Actors

An *Actor* is any object that can be added to a Level. Consider the objects on the left side of the Unreal Editor when you first start a project. If you click on the cube, for example, and drag it into the Level, it will become an Actor within the Level.

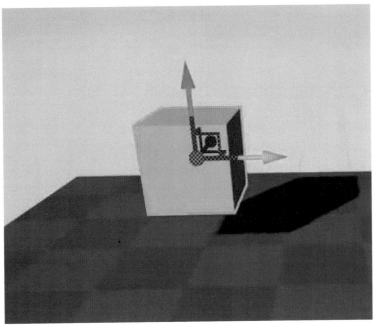

Figure 2.3.1 – This cube is an Actor within the Level

Actors can be physical, visible objects within the Level, such as the cube, but they don't have to be. For example, there is something called the *Player Start Actor*. Wherever this Actor is placed within the Level is where the player will start when the Level begins. Even though the Player Start Actor isn't a physical object within the Level, it is still considered to be an Actor.

The Static Mesh Actor

The *Static Mesh Actor* is one of the most common types of Actors used to construct Levels in the Unreal Editor. If you're not familiar, "mesh" is a 3D modeling term, and simply refers to a 3D object. When you're playing a game, pretty much every object you see in the game will be a mesh. For example, you may see tree meshes, bird meshes, table meshes, chair meshes, and so on.

Static meshes refer to meshes with no moving parts. For example, the cube and the other geometric shapes in that list.

In the Starter Content that comes with the Unreal Engine, you have some Static Meshes in the form of furniture and some basic architectural objects.

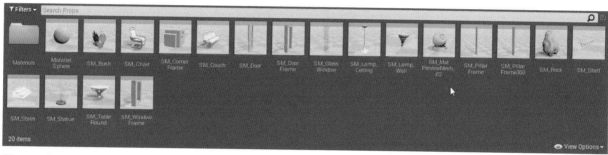

Figure 2.3.2 – Some static meshes are included in the Starter Content

So you have some Meshes to start with, but the vast majority of meshes used in games are created in external 3D modeling applications, such as Maya, 3D Studio Max, Blender, and so on, and then imported into the Unreal Editor. If you're not a 3D-modeling artist, don't despair; there is lots of great content available on the Internet for you to use, for free or for a price, and the final chapter of this book will show you where you can find some of that content.

Geometry Brushes

A *Geometry Brush*, or simply "Brush" for short, is an Actor used to represent 3D space. There is a Box Brush, a Cone Brush, and so on. This is very similar to a Mesh, but there are a few key differences. These differences will be discussed in greater detail in a later chapter, so, for now, just know the following:

- Brushes are only used for basic geometric shapes while Meshes can be crafted into objects with a high level of detail.

- Brushes are useful for quick level design but are less memory-efficient than Meshes. Therefore, Brushes are generally used to prototype Levels early on, and are then replaced with better-looking and better-performing Meshes for the final project.

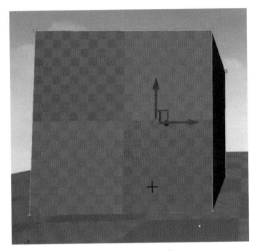

Figure 2.3.3 – A Box Brush

Materials

Before moving on to the next Actor, you should know about a property that is common to both Meshes and Brushes - the Material of the Actor. A *Material* in Unreal Engine is an Asset you can apply to a surface to make that surface, and thus the geometry behind that surface, look like it's made out of a certain substance. For example, if you apply a wood Material to a Cube Mesh, it will look like a wooden cube.

Figure 2.3.4 – A wood Material has been applied to this Cube Mesh

Meshes that are imported into the Unreal Editor may already have one or more Materials applied to them that get imported in alongside them. But you can replace these Materials if you wish.

The Light Actor

A *Light Actor* in the Unreal Engine is used to represent visible light in the real world. Thanks to a lot of complex, mathematical algorithms that the Unreal Engine uses, it will behave much like light does in the real world. It will make objects that it hits more visible, depending on the intensity of the Light and the Material of the object. It will reflect off the surface of objects and light up other objects indirectly. It will cast a shadow if a visible, opaque object is in its path, and so on.

Lights will be discussed in greater detail in a later chapter, but for now, just know that Light Actors are used to represent only the light itself, and not any of the objects from which the light emanates from. For example, if you wanted a working flashlight in your Level, you would need to combine a Light Actor with a Static Mesh Actor that looked like a flashlight. You would place the Light Actor at one end of the flashlight to make it look like the light was coming out of the flashlight.

Summary of Actors

To summarize, an Actor is any object you can place and move about your Level. Brushes are a type of geometric Actor used to quickly prototype and structure a Level. Static Meshes are a type of Actor that are used to represent realistic looking objects in your Level. Materials can be applied to the surfaces of Brushes and Static Meshes to make them look as if they are made out of that type of material. Lights are a type of Actor used to light the whole thing up.

2.4 Chapter 2 Quiz

1. In the Unreal Engine, what is the name of the unit that stores all the information for an individual game?

2. Describe a scenario where would you need to use the Browse button in the Project Browser to find a project.

3. Describe a scenario where you would need to use the Refresh button in order for a project to appear in the Project Browser.

4. In the Unreal Engine, what can be defined as a collection of objects and their properties that together define an area of gameplay?

5. True or False: Major game releases rarely contain hundreds of Levels.

6. Anything you can open or add to your game within the Content Browser can be described as a what?

7. Any object that can be added to a Level is called a what?

8. True or False: Only physical, visible objects within a Level are considered Actors.

9. What is a four-letter technical term for a digital 3D object?

10. What do you call a mesh with no moving parts?

11. What kind of Actor, used to represent 3D space, is useful for prototyping your Levels?

12. What is an Asset you can apply to a surface to make that surface look like it's made out of a certain substance?

13. True or False: Light Actors are used to represent objects that emit light.

Answers

1. project

2. If you downloaded a project from the Internet and saved it to a location other than Unreal's installation directory.

3. If you downloaded a project from the Internet and saved it in Unreal's installation directory.

4. Level

5. False. It is not uncommon for a major release to contains hundreds of Levels.

6. Asset

7. Actor

8. False

9. mesh

10. static mesh

11. Brush

12. Material

13. False. Light Actors are only used for the light itself. You would use a mesh to represent the object that is emitting the light.

3

The Level Editor

3.1 Level Editor Overview

This section will give a basic overview of the Level Editor without going into too much detail. First, we will spend a few moments discussing some terminology which can be confusing.

Unreal Engine vs the Unreal Editor

The Unreal Engine is an application that is used to run games. It's a program that has algorithms for determining how objects are rendered frame by frame, how lighting should affect them, and so on. The Unreal Editor is an application for *creating* games that can run on the Unreal Engine. So that's what you're learning in this book - how to create games with the Unreal Editor that can be played using the Unreal Engine.

When you hit the Play button to play your game, the Unreal Editor is using the Unreal Engine to run the game. To summarize, the Unreal Editor is used for *creating* games, while the Unreal Engine is used for *running* those games.

Unreal Editor vs the Level Editor

The Unreal Editor has several sub-editors within it, and one of those sub-editors is the Level Editor. What can be confusing about this, however, is that the Level Editor essentially acts as the home screen for the Unreal Editor. So the main window of the Unreal Editor is the Level Editor itself. All of the other sub-editors will open in their own separate windows. For example, if you double-click on a Material, it will open the Material Editor in a separate window.

Panels of the Level Editor

The large rectangle in the middle is the *Viewport*. The thin strip above that is the *Toolbar*. At the bottom of the screen is the *Content Browser*. On the left side of the screen is the *Modes Panel*. On the right side of the screen is the *World Outliner* at the top, and below that, the *Details Panel*.

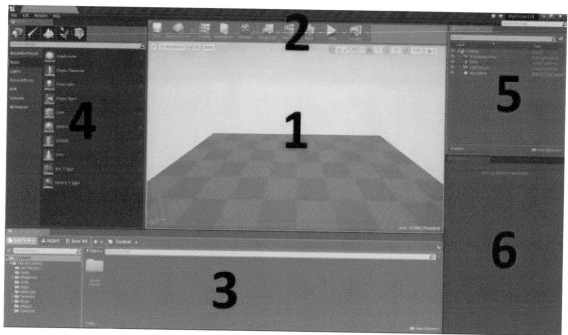

Figure 3.1.1 – The panels of the Level Editor - 1. Viewport 2. Toolbar 3. Content Browser 4. Modes Panel 5. World Outliner 6. Details Panel

Keep in mind that these panels can be moved and resized, and also that this is just the default layout of the current release and could change in future releases.

The *Viewport* is used to give you a visual representation of your game. You will see a representation of the environment you create, along with characters and objects that players will see in the game. You will also be able to see certain objects in the Viewport that won't be visible when playing the game, such as cameras, event triggers, and invisible barriers. You can also manipulate objects directly through the Viewport.

Figure 3.1.2 — The Viewport

The *Toolbar* is a strip of buttons meant to give you quick access to common and/or important functions, such as saving, changing settings, or playing your game.

Figure 3.1.3 — The Toolbar

The *Content Browser* is for storing and organizing content that you can add to your game. This includes content such as Meshes, Materials, music, sound effects, visual effects, and more. Some types of content can be created directly within the Unreal Editor. But you can also create content outside of the Unreal Editor and then import it in. For example, you could create a motorcycle using third-party 3D-modeling software, and then use the Content Browser to import the motorcycle into your project. There is also a lot of already made content available on the Internet, for free or for a price, that you can download and then import into the Content Browser.

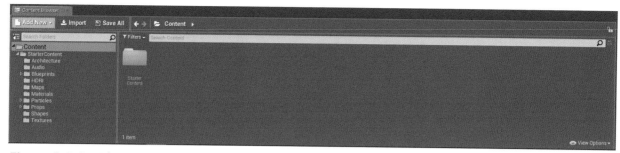

Figure 3.1.4 – The Content Browser

The *Modes Panel* allows you to change the mode of the Level Editor to various modes that make it easier to perform certain tasks. These tasks include dragging and dropping objects into your Level, adding color and texture to those objects, modifying the geometry of those objects, editing the landscape of your Level, and adding foliage, meaning plant life, to your Level.

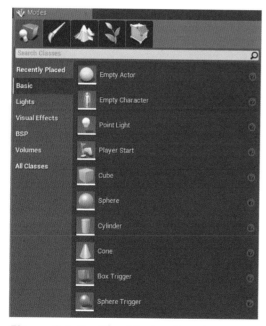

Figure 3.1.5 – The Modes Panel

The *World Outliner* is used to list and group the objects in your Level in a way that makes them easy to find when you want to select and edit them.

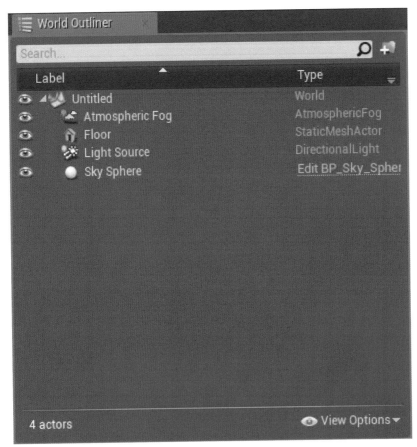

Figure 3.1.6 – The World Outliner

The *Details Panel* allows you to view and edit the details of whatever object is currently selected, such as the object's size and location.

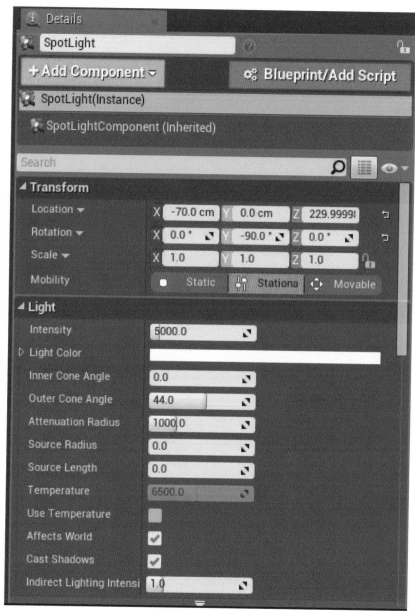

Figure 3.1.7 – The Details Panel

Customizing the Interface

The Unreal Editor gives you a great deal of control over how the interface looks. One thing you can do is resize the individual panels. To do this, simply click on the edge between two panels and drag, and you can make them any size you wish.

You also have the option to move panels around. If you click on the tab of the panel and drag, you can drag it to wherever you want on the screen.

You can also choose which panels are open at any given time. To close a panel, simply click on the "X" on the right side of the panel's tab. To open a panel, go to the menu bar, and under Window, select the panel you wish to open.

Finally, you can choose to show or hide the tabs of each panel. To hide the tab, right-click on it, and choose *Hide Tab*. To show the tab, click on the yellow triangle in the upper-left corner of the panel. You may want to have all the tabs showing while you are still learning the names of the panels, and then once you have them memorized, close the tabs in order to have a little more screen room to work with.

3.2 Place Mode

The Modes Panel has five different modes. To select the mode you want to work in, simply click on one of the five icons at the top of the Modes Panel, or hold down the *Shift* key and press either the *1, 2, 3, 4,* or *5* key depending on which mode you want to select.

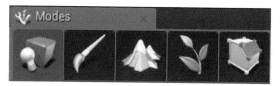

Figure 3.2.1 – The five modes of the Modes Panel

The first mode is called *Place Mode*. Place Mode can be selected by pressing *Shift+1* or by clicking on the first icon, the one with the brown box and light bulb.

Place Mode is used to place Actors into your Level. The Content Browser is also used for placing Actors but there are a few key differences. Place Mode is used for simple, common, generic Actors, while the Actors in the Content Browser tend to be more complex. Also, the list of Actors in Place Mode remains static. You cannot add new Actors to the Place Mode panel, while in the Content Browser, you can import content created outside of the Unreal Editor into your project or create new ones.

To use Place Mode to place an Actor into a Level, simply click on the Actor and drag it into the Viewport. To delete an Actor from the Level, press the *Delete* key when that Actor is selected.

Place Mode Tabs

Place Mode is divided into tabs of different groupings of Actors. Starting with the *Basic* tab, the Basic tab simply contains 10 of the most commonly used Actors.

Figure 3.2.2 – The tabs of Place Mode

Above the Basic tab is the *Recently Placed* tab. This will be a list of Actors that you have recently placed into your Level. This is useful when you are going to be working with a small set of the same types of Actors for a while. In that scenario you would be able to just keep the Recently Placed tab open, and drag and drop everything from there, without having to switch between all of the other tabs.

Below the Basic tab is the *Lights* tab. As mentioned earlier in the book, a Light in the Unreal Engine is an Actor that is meant to represent the light projecting from some source.

Then we have *Visual Effects*, which as its name suggests, contains Actors that add a variety of effects to your Level.

The *BSP* tab contains the Geometry Brushes that were briefly introduced earlier. BSP stands for "Binary Space Partitioning" but that's not important to know. Just know that this is the Brushes tab.

The *Volumes* tab is used to define gameplay volumes. A Volume is a 3D area of space that is invisible to the player and serves a specific purpose depending on its type. For example, a Blocking Volume will prevent Actors from being able to enter that Volume, a Pain Causing Volume will cause damage to an Actor who enters that volume, and so on.

Last, is the *All Classes* tab, which contains all the Actors from the other tabs, plus some additional Actors not found in any of the other tabs, either because they are less common or just didn't fit nicely into one of the other groups. The list is somewhat long, so you may want to use the search bar above. By typing into the search bar, you can quickly narrow down the results to what you are looking for.

3.3 Navigating Within the Viewport

There are three main ways to navigate in the Viewport.

Mouse Navigation

The first way to navigate the Viewport is by *mouse navigation*. Try holding down the left mouse button (LMB) and dragging the mouse. This allows you to move the camera forward or backwards and to rotate it left and right. There is no way to move up and down with this movement. It is only for travelling along the X and Y axes. Also, you cannot move directly left or right with this movement, you can only rotate left and right.

Now hold the LMB and the right mouse button (RMB) at the same time and drag the mouse. This will allow you to move directly left and right and up and down. Also, if you have a middle mouse button, you can hold that down instead of the left and right mouse buttons, to achieve the same effect.

Finally, try holding down just the RMB and dragging the mouse. This won't move the camera along any axes but what it does do is allow you to rotate the camera in any direction so you can look at the scene from whatever angle you wish.

WASD Navigation

The second way to navigate the Viewport is to use *WASD navigation*. This is used to move around the Viewport in a way that more closely mimics the controls commonly used when playing a standard first-person game using the mouse and keyboard. It's called WASD because it uses the *W*, *A*, *S* and *D* keys on the keyboard, and a few of the keys surrounding those keys.

To use WASD navigation, you will need to keep the RMB clicked the whole time. This will allow you to rotate the camera in any direction using the mouse, as discussed before, but also, when the RMB is clicked, the WASD keys will cause movement. Use the *W*, *A*, *S* and *D* keys themselves to move the camera forward, backwards, left, and right. Use the keys *Q* and *E* to move the camera up and down. Use the keys *Z* and *C* to zoom the camera in and out. Note that zooming is only temporary. Once you let go of the RMB, the zoom will go back to default.

Focusing

Before learning the third way of navigating the Viewport, you should know about *focusing* - a very simple yet powerful feature of the Viewport window. Focusing is useful in conjunction with the third navigation method and on its own.

To focus, press the *F* key, and it will focus the camera on whatever object is selected. This is useful in large Levels and Levels with many Actors. In these cases, it is often much easier to find the Actor in the World Outliner list and then press *F* to go straight to it in the Viewport, rather than trying to hunt for the Actor visually in the Viewport.

Maya Navigation

The third way to navigate the Viewport is to use *Maya navigation*. Maya refers to a popular 3D modeling program in which these controls are used. The three controls in Maya navigation are performed by holding down the *Alt* key.

The first Maya control is done by holding the *Alt* key, along with the LMB, and dragging the mouse. This will "tumble" or "orbit" the camera around a single point of interest. However, even if an Actor is selected, it won't actually use that Actor as the point of interest. To do that, you must press *F* to focus on the Actor.

The second Maya control is performed by holding the *Alt* key and the RMB and dragging the mouse. This will "dolly" or "zoom" the camera toward, and away from, a single point of interest. Again, press *F* to focus on an object first, in order to dolly directly towards and away from it.

The final Maya control is performed by holding down the *Alt* key and the MMB and dragging the mouse. This will cause the camera to "track", or "pan", up, down, left, and right.

Camera Speed

To adjust the speed at which the camera moves about the Level, adjust the camera speed slider in the upper-right corner of the Viewport. If you have a very large Level and want to be able to move about it quickly, you can set the camera speed up to an 8 and your camera will move very quickly. Conversely, if you need a fine level of control over the camera speed, you can set it down as low as a 1, and it will move very slowly. A setting of 4 is the default speed.

Figure 3.3.1 – Setting the Camera Speed

3.4 Moving, Rotating, and Scaling Actors

Moving, rotating, and scaling Actors within the Viewport is performed by using the Move, Rotate, and Scale tools. When you select an Actor, you will automatically be ready to use one of the tools, depending on which of the three are selected at that moment. To see which tool is selected, look at the first three icons in upper-right of the Viewport. From left to right, these three icons represent the Move, Rotate, and Scale tools. Whichever tool is currently selected will have an orange background.

Figure 3.4.1 – The Move, Rotate, and Scale tools

To change between the tools, click on their icons, or use the shortcut keys *W*, *E*, and *R* to switch between them. The *W*, *E*, and *R* keys are in a row on the keyboard and activate the Move, Rotate, and Scale tools in the same order as those icons appear on the screen. So the *W* key will activate the Move Tool, the *E* key will activate the Rotate Tool, and the *R* key will activate the Scale Tool. If you forget what the shortcut keys are, just hover over the icon and it will tell you in parentheses at the end of the description.

Move Tool

When the Move Tool is active and an Actor is selected, three different-colored arrows will appear on the Actor. These three arrows are aligned with the X, Y, and Z axes of the Level. To move an Actor in just the X direction, left-click on the red arrow, and use the mouse to move the Actor back and forth in that direction. No matter what direction you drag the mouse, the Actor will only move along the X-axis when the red arrow is held. To move an Actor along the Y-axis, select the green arrow instead. To move an Actor up and down, along the Z-axis, use the blue arrow.

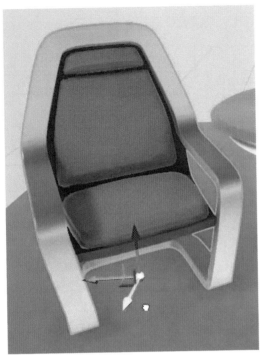

Figure 3.4.2 – A Static Mesh being moved with the Move Tool

To move an Actor in two dimensions, click on the connector between those axes. For example, let's say you already have a chair Mesh perfectly aligned with a floor, and you don't want to mess that up, but you do want to change where the chair is located otherwise. In that case, you would click on the connector between the X and Y axes and then you could move the chair forward, backwards, left, and right, but not vertical in any direction, so that it remains perfectly aligned with the floor.

To move an Actor in all three dimensions at once, select the white sphere in the middle of the arrows and drag the mouse.

If multiple Actors are selected, they will all move at once. To select multiple Actors, once the first Actor is selected, hold down the *Ctrl* button and continue to left-click on each additional Actor you wish to select. Note that the Move Tool will only be visible on the last Actor selected, but in the World Outliner all the selected Actors will be highlighted.

If the *Shift* key is held while using the Move Tool, the camera will move in tandem with the Actor. This is useful if you want to move your Actor while keeping the camera focused on it in the exact same way or if you want to move the Actor some distance off screen and don't want to have to keep moving back and forth between moving the Actor and camera. Note that this only works when moving in one or two dimensions.

To make a copy of an Actor, you can select that Actor and press *Ctrl+W*. Alternatively, when you are using the Move Tool, if you hold down the *Alt* key, when you hold and drag along an axis, instead of moving the Actor, it will make a copy of that Actor which you will now be moving along that axis. You can hold down the *Alt* key to drag out several copies of an Actor.

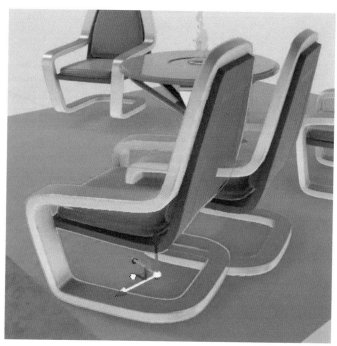

Figure 3.4.3 – An Actor being copied using the Move Tool

Rotate Tool

Pressing the *E* key will activate the Rotate Tool. Using the Rotate Tool, you can rotate an Actor around any of the three axes. Clicking on the red arc and dragging the mouse will rotate an Actor around the X-axis. The green arc rotates around the Y-axis. The blue arc rotates around the Z-axis.

Figure 3.4.4 – The Rotate Tool

Similar to the Move Tool, if the *Alt* key is held when dragging the mouse, it will instead make a copy of the Actor which will then rotate out of the original Actor.

Scale Tool

Pressing the *R* key will activate the Scale Tool. The Scale Tool allows you to make your Actors bigger or smaller.

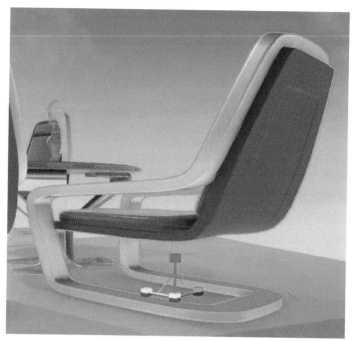

Figure 3.4.5 – The Scale Tool scaling a Static Mesh along the X-axis

Using the same concept as the Move Tool, you can increase or decrease the size along just one axis at a time, or adjust the size two dimensions at a time by clicking and dragging on one of the connectors between the axes. You can change the overall size of the Actor uniformly, by clicking on the white square in the middle and dragging the mouse.

World Space vs Local Space

An important concept you should understand is that of "world space vs local space". Look at the box to the right of the Move, Rotate, and Scale tools. If that box displays an icon of the Earth, it means that the axes of an Actor will be oriented to *world space*. If it displays an icon of a grey cube, Actors will be oriented to *local space*. Clicking on the icon or using the shortcut *Ctrl+~* will toggle between the two settings.

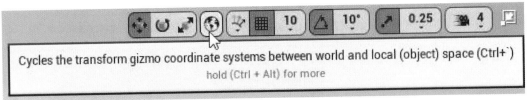

Figure 3.4.6 – An icon of the Earth means that Actors will be oriented to world space

Let's say the Move Tool is active and Actors are currently oriented to world space. That means that no matter which way an Actor has been previously rotated, the arrows of the Move Tool will still point in the same direction, and thus the Move Tool will still move the Actor in the same direction relative to the world.

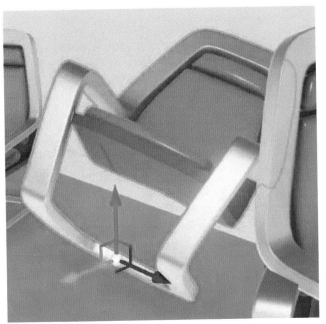

Figure 3.4.7 – Actor oriented to world space

In local space, however, the direction of the arrows depend on the rotation of that particular Actor. In other words, world space makes the axes point relative to the world, while local space makes the axes point relative to the Actor.

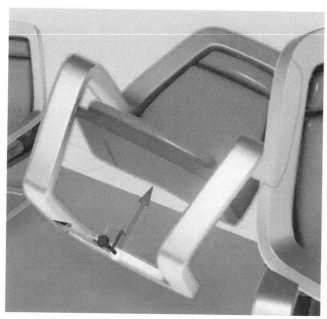

Figure 3.4.8 – Actor oriented to local space

The same concept applies to the Rotate Tool. In local space, an Actor will rotate around the locally-oriented axes. This setting does not apply, however, to the Scale Tool. The Scale Tool will always be in local space, and it won't allow you to toggle when the Scale Tool is selected.

3.5 Snapping

Snapping is a technique used to perfectly align Actors with one another. There are several different ways of using snapping.

End Key

The first method involves using the *End* key. When the *End* key is pressed while an Actor is selected, it will snap that Actor directly onto the nearest surface. This is useful for quickly aligning objects, such as getting Actors to sit directly on a floor.

Surface Snapping

Another way of using snapping is called *Surface Snapping*. Clicking on the icon to the right of the world space icon will bring up a small pop-up where you can turn on Surface Snapping. With Surface Snapping on, when the Move Tool is used to move an Actor around in three dimensions, any time it gets close to the surface of another Actor, it will snap the selected Actor to the surface of the nearby Actor.

Figure 3.5.1 – Surface Snapping turned on

Note that this only works when moving the object in three dimensions. It doesn't work when moving Actors around in just one or two dimensions at a time. In other words, you need to be dragging the Actor around by the white sphere in the middle for Surface Snapping to work.

Surface snapping has a couple of settings you can adjust to change how it behaves. The first setting is called *Rotate to Surface Normal* and it is set to "On" by default. The following example will illustrate how this works.

Imagine there is an Actor that was rotated such that its bottom surface was no longer in alignment with the surface of the floor. With Surface Snapping on and Rotate to Surface Normal off, when the Actor gets close to the floor, it will snap to the floor, but it will keep the Actor at the same rotation it was without attempting to rotate it to align with the floor.

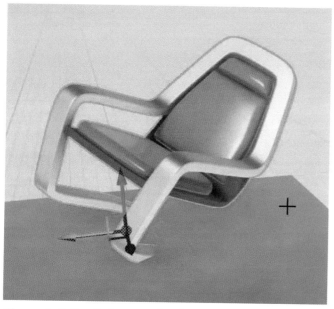

Figure 3.5.2 – Rotate to Surface Normal was off when this chair was snapped to the floor

However, with Rotate to Surface Normal on, when the Actor snaps to the floor, it will also be rotated so that its bottom surface is perfectly aligned with the surface of the floor.

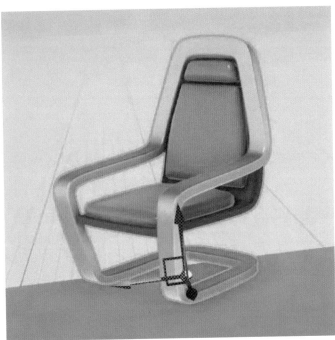

Figure 3.5.3 – Rotate to Surface Normal was on when this chair was snapped to the floor

The second setting of Surface Snapping that you can adjust is the *Surface Offset*. This tells the Editor how far away the surfaces of the two Actors should be when they snap together. A value of 0 will cause Actors to be directly touching when they snap. A value of 20 would cause Actors to be 20 centimeters apart after snapping.

Grid Snapping

You can also align objects by using *Grid Snapping*. While Surface Snapping is useful for aligning objects that are close to one another, Grid Snapping is useful for aligning objects across distances.

Clicking the icon to the right of the Surface Snapping icon will toggle Grid Snapping on and off. With Grid Snapping on, as an Actor is moved, it will only be able to move it in the increments that the grid is divided into. The Actor will "snap" to each line of the grid and can't move a smaller amount than that. With Grid Snapping off, an Actor can be moved any distance.

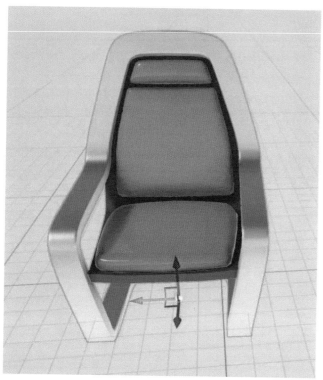

Figure 3.5.4 – With Grid Snapping on, this chair will snap to each line of the grid when moved

Snap Size

To the right of the Grid Snapping icon, is a box where you can adjust the *Snap Size*. This will change the number of units that the Actor can move at a time. Set at 10, the Actor will move in increments of 10 units at a time.

Figure 3.5.5 — Setting the Snap Size

Note that the number of lines visible on the grid at any given time is dependent on the Snap Size that is set. Set at 10, the grid is actually only displaying one out of every ten lines it contains. At a Snap Size of 1, every line on the grid will become visible.

Grid Units

In the Unreal Editor, 1 grid unit represents 1 centimeter in your game. So whenever you see a number in the Unreal Editor meant to represent a unit of distance, you can think of that number in centimeters. For example, with Snap Size set to 10, an Actor moved within the Viewport will move 10 "in-game" centimeters at a time.

Rotation Snapping

Just like with the Move Tool, snapping can be turned on or off for the Rotate Tool. To toggle *Rotation Snapping*, click on the icon to the right of the Snap Size icon. With Rotation Snapping on, an Actor can be rotated in specified increments along a *Rotation Grid*, with those increments being measured in degrees. So the Unreal Editor measures distances in centimeters and it measures rotation in degrees.

You can choose how many degrees the Actor should rotate each time, by clicking the icon to the right of the Rotation Snapping icon. Set to 10, an Actor will rotate in increments of 10 degrees.

Scale Snapping

Just like with Move and Rotate, you can toggle *Scale Snapping* on or off. To do so, click on the icon to the right of the rotation degrees icon.

To change the increment that is scaled by, click the icon to the right of the Scale Snapping icon. With the Scale Tool, the increment is a multiplier. For example, if 0.25 is selected, and you increment an Actor one size larger, its size will increase by 0.25 times its current size. In other words, its size will increase by 25%. If you make it smaller, it will decrease by 25% at a time. With a setting of 0.5, it would increase or decrease in increments of 50%, and so on.

3.6 Different Ways to View Your Level

This section will show you different ways you can view your Level, that can make level design easier, depending on the situation.

Immersive Mode

Pressing *F11* will fullscreen the Viewport. This is what Unreal calls *Immersive Mode*. Pressing *F11* again will exit fullscreen.

View Modes

Another way you can view your Level differently is by changing the *View Mode*. To change the View Mode, hover over the second-to-last box in the upper-left corner of the Viewport and click on one of the selections from the menu that appears.

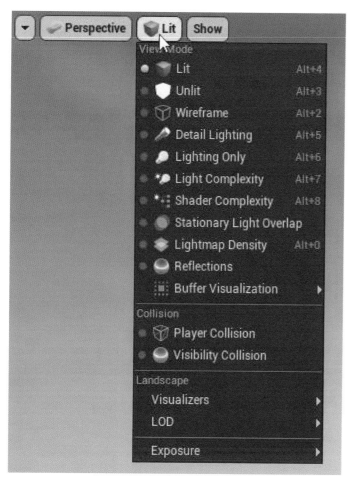

Figure 3.6.1 – View Modes

Most of these View Modes are for viewing subtle details in regards to lighting that are beyond the scope of a beginner's book, so only the first three will be covered. These are Lit, Unlit, and Wireframe.

Lit Mode

Lit is the default View Mode of the Level Editor and is for viewing the Level with full lighting and rendering, similar to what the player will see in-game.

Unlit Mode

Unlit is for viewing the Level without the lighting having any impact on what you see. In essence, this allows you to see the base colors of all objects without the amount of light or shadow affecting that color. Unlit is also useful for working in Levels or areas of Levels where the lighting would otherwise be too dark to easily see what you're doing.

Figure 3.6.2 – A Level in Unlit Mode

Wireframe Mode

Wireframe mode allows you to see just the edges of the polygons of the objects in your Level. This can be helpful for aligning objects, visualizing the overall structure of something, and, in general, just giving you a more architectural view of your Level.

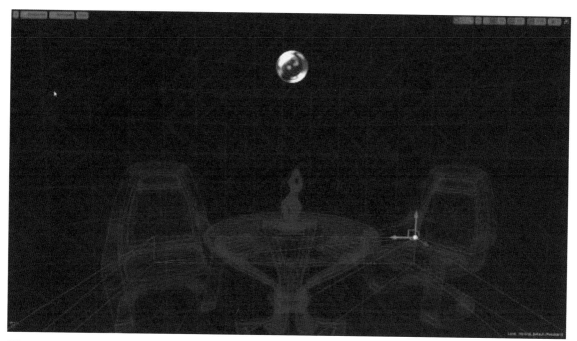

Figure 3.6.3 – A Level in Wireframe Mode

Orthographic Views

To the left of the View Modes menu is a menu that allows you to change between the default 3D perspective view of the Level, to an orthographic view of the Level. There are several different orthographic views to choose from, but they all share two common traits. The first is that they default to a wireframe view mode, although you can still change the View Mode if you want.

The main thing about orthographic views is that they are meant to be a 2-dimensional view of your Level, rather than a 3-dimensional view. For example, in the "Top" view, your vision is directly parallel with the Z-axis, so it is as if you are looking directly down at your Level, and only seeing the X and Y axes. Conversely, in "Bottom" view, you are looking directly up at the Level.

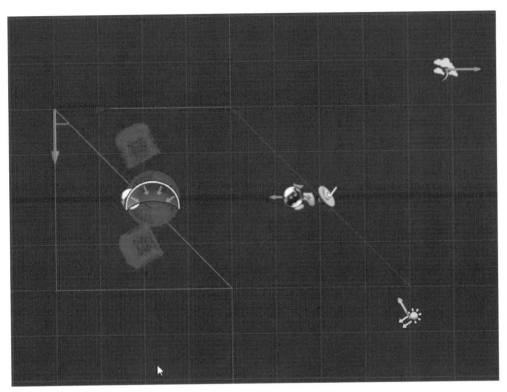

Figure 3.6.4 – A Level in Orthographic Top view

In the "Left" and "Right" views, you are looking down the X-axis and only seeing the Y and Z axes. In the "Front" and "Back" views, you are looking down the Y-axis and only seeing the X and Z axes.

So each of the orthographic views has the point of vision coming from a different place, but it will always be directly along an axis, giving you a 2-dimensional view.

Orthographic views are useful for aligning the objects in your Level in just two dimensions at a time. When paired with the wireframe view mode, the idea is to get a 2D architectural view of your Level.

When working in orthographic views, the navigation is a bit different than the perspective view. When in an orthographic view, holding down the LMB and dragging is used for drawing a selection box that you can use to select one or more objects. To navigate, hold down the RMB and drag to pan the Viewport camera, or hold the left and right mouse buttons down and drag, in order to zoom the camera in and out. So LMB to select, RMB to pan, and both mouse buttons to zoom.

Show Flags

Another way to change the view of your Level is by toggling the various *Show Flags* on and off. Show Flags can be toggled using the checkboxes found in the icon to the right of the View Modes icon. Show Flags tell the Editor whether or not to show various types of Actors or effects in the Viewport.

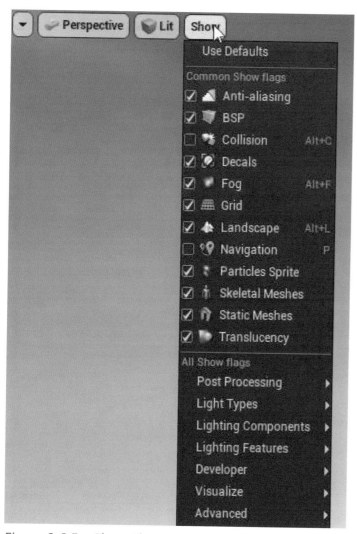

Figure 3.6.5 – Show Flags

For example, if you uncheck the "Static Meshes" Show Flag, all of the Static Meshes in the Level will disappear from the Viewport. This doesn't delete the Static Meshes from the Viewport, it only makes them invisible for the time being. It also doesn't make them invisible in the game, only in the Viewport.

Show Flags are useful for temporarily removing some of the clutter from view, once your Levels start to get complex. Even when they're not complex, sometimes you may have one type of object blocking another type and it's just easier to temporarily get the one out of the way.

Game View

If you press the *G* key, you can toggle the Viewport in and out of *Game View*. When the Viewport is in Game View, it will hide all Actors and icons that are invisible in-game. So the Player Start Actor, for example, will be hidden, along with the icons for your Light Actors, and so on. Game View is meant to show you in the Viewport, exactly what the player would see from that perspective in the game.

Piloting Actors Within the Viewport

Sometimes it is useful when placing Actors, especially Camera and Light Actors, to see from the perspective of the Actor itself. This makes it easier to have the Actor point at the exact location you want it to point at.

For example, if you place a Light Actor in a Level, and want it to shine directly on a table Mesh, you can pilot the Light in order to more easily aim it directly at the table.

To pilot an Actor, right-click on it, then look for an airplane icon and the text "Pilot [Actor]" (a Spot Light Actor will say "Pilot Spot Light"). Alternatively, select the Actor and use the shortcut *Ctrl+Shift+P*.

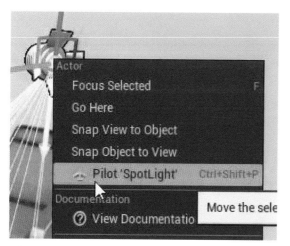

Figure 3.6.6 – Piloting an Actor in the Viewport

3.7 Content Browser

The *Content Browser*, just like Place Mode of the Modes panel, can be used to drag and drop Actors into a Level. However, while Place Mode contains a list of generic, built-in Actors for you to use, the Content Browser can be used to create Actors, or to import in Actors created outside of the Unreal Editor.

Sources Panel and Asset Window

Most of the space of the Content Browser is taken up by two panels. The smaller panel on the left is the *Sources Panel*. The Sources Panel contains the folder directory for the Content Browser. To the right of the Sources Panel is the *Asset Window*. When a folder is selected in the Sources Panel, that folder will open in the Asset Window. The Asset Window will contain both the sub-folders of that folder and, unlike the Sources Panel, it will also contain the files, or Assets, within that folder.

The Sources Panel is useful for navigating through the folders without the clutter of the files themselves, but, if you just want to work with the Asset Window alone, you have the option to hide the Sources Panel. Pressing the button in the upper-left will toggle the visibility of the Sources Panel on and off.

The Sources Panel contains a search box that can be used to find specific folders. The Asset Window contains a search box that can be used to find specific Assets. For example, you could type "lamp" to search for all Assets with "lamp" in their name.

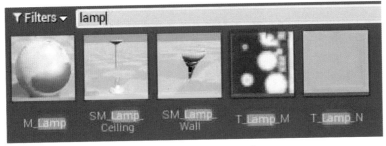

Figure 3.7.1 – Searching the Asset Window

The Asset Window also has a Filters menu that can be used to find content of a certain type. For example, clicking "Static Mesh" will show all the Static Meshes, and only the Static Meshes, within the current folder and its sub-folders. Clicking on the "Reset Filters" button will clear out any filters currently being applied.

The search and filter functions can be combined. Let's say you were specifically looking for Static Meshes of lamps. By typing "lamp" into the search box and applying the Static Mesh filter, it will narrow down the results to only Static Mesh files with "lamp" in the name.

Back Button and Forward Button

Above the Sources Panel and Asset Window, there is a back button and a forward button. These work just like the back and forward buttons in Windows or in a web browser. You can use them to go back to the last so many folders you were in, and then forward again if you wish. So if you go to a "FirstPerson" folder, and then a "MyImports" folder, and then a "StarterContent" folder, and then hit the back button, it will take you back to the MyImports folder. If you hit the back button again, it will take you back to the FirstPerson folder. Now if you hit forward it will go to the MyImports folder, and then to the StarterContent folder again.

Breadcrumbs

To the right of the back and forward buttons are the breadcrumbs. You've probably seen this kind of navigation layout before even if you've never heard the term, but the basic idea is to show you the direct path from the root folder down to the folder you're in.

Figure 3.7.2 - Breadcrumbs

Each folder in the folder path will have its own button. Clicking on a button will take you directly to that folder. Clicking on the arrow icon to the right of the folder name will bring up a list of all the sub-folders, which can also be navigated to directly by clicking on.

Add New Button

In the upper-left corner of the Content Browser is a green *Add New* button which can be used to add a variety of assets to the Content Browser. For example, clicking on *New Folder* will add a new folder within the current folder.

Figure 3.7.3 – Add New button

At the very top of the Add New menu is *Add Feature or Content Pack*. This gives you the chance to add in some of the content that is available when you first create a project. For example, clicking on "First Person" will add folders containing some basic content for creating a first-person game. Note, however, that unlike when you choose the First-Person template when starting a project, this method doesn't automatically add and hook up any content into your Level, it just adds it to the Content Browser. From there you can drag and drop the content into your Level as you choose.

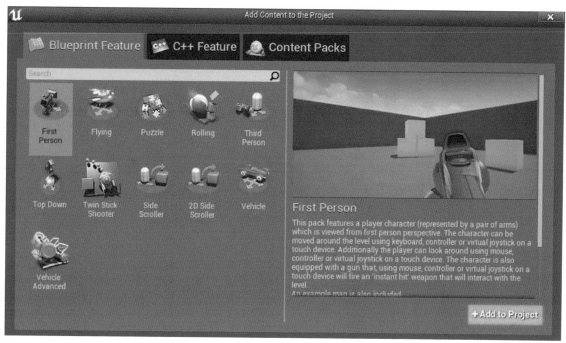

Figure 3.7.4 – Add Feature or Content Pack

The Content Packs tab gives you the option to add the Starter Content into the Content Browser if you hadn't already done so when creating the project. There is also an option for Starter Content specifically for mobile devices.

Import Button

To the right of the Add New button is the *Import* button. If you have a file on your computer that you want to import into the current project, all you need to do is click the Import button, and select the file, and it will import that file directly into whatever folder you're currently in, in the Content Browser. Alternatively, you can simply drag and drop files from your computer directly into the Content Browser.

Save All Button

To the right of the Import button is the *Save All* button. When the icon of an image in the Content Browser has an asterisk in its lower-left, this means that this Asset hasn't been saved. By clicking the Save All button, it will bring up a window that lists all the unsaved Assets in the Content Browser and allows you to unselect any if you don't want to save them. Once "Save Selected" is clicked, the asterisk will go away, indicating that the Asset has been saved and has no new modifications.

View Options

In the bottom-right of the Content Browser is the View Options button. As the name implies, if you click this button, you will get a menu of options related to viewing the content in the Content Browser.

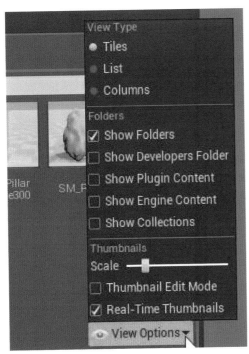

Figure 3.7.5 – View Options in the Content Browser

Tiles vs List vs Columns

For example, you can change the way the files are displayed. By default, it is set to *Tiles*, which will display the files with large icons in a grid formation. *List* will make the files display using smaller icons and larger text and will be positioned one per row. *Columns* will display additional information for each Asset.

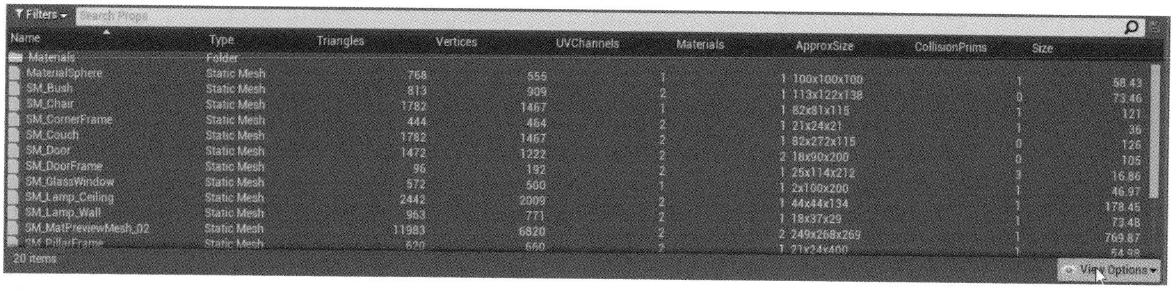

Figure 3.7.6 – Assets in List view

Show Folders

By default, folders in the Asset Window are displayed, but by unchecking *Show Folders*, only the Assets will show, and not the folders.

Show Developers Folders

The next option in the menu is *Show Developers Folders*. Sometimes you might want to experiment with things without risking messing up your game you've been working on, or you may just prefer to keep unfinished assets separate from your game until they've been completed. In these situations, you want a sandbox environment you can work in that's separate from the rest of your content. This is what the Developers Folders are for.

If you click Show Developers Folders, you will see an additional entry in the Sources Panel labeled "Developers." If you expand that, you should see another folder with your name on it that you can use to store your test assets. If there were multiple people working on a project, each person would have their own folder. This is so everyone's test assets are not only kept separate from the game but also separate from each other, to reduce unnecessary clutter.

Show Plugins Content

The next checkbox is *Show Plugins Content*. Checking this will allow you to see the content used by the third-party plugins that have been added onto the Unreal Engine. For the most part, this content is just the source code for these plugins, so, you're probably not ever going to have a need to access it. In fact, even if you know how to code, you shouldn't try to modify any of this content unless you really know what you're doing.

Show Engine Content

The same goes for *Show Engine Content*. This will allow you to see, and thus modify, the source code for the Unreal Engine itself, which isn't recommended.

Show Collections

The next option is *Show Collections*. If enabled, a Collections panel will appear over in the bottom-half of the Sources Panel. *Collections* are a way to help you organize your Assets by placing them into groups. Often, organizing your assets into a logical folder structure is enough, but that can only go so far.

For example, let's say you wanted to have a grouping of all your chair Assets. You could make a folder called "Chairs" and move all the chairs into it. But what if you also wanted to group all of the yellow objects? You could make a folder called "Yellow," but then you would have to choose whether to put the yellow chair in the Chairs folder or the Yellow folder. And you don't want to have to try and track and maintain multiple copies of your Assets either.

The solution is to use Collections, because when you add an Asset to a Collection you are really only adding a shortcut to that Asset in the Collection and not the Asset itself. So you can add an Asset to multiple Collections without having to move or make a copy of the Asset itself. You can make a Collection called "Chairs" and add a chair to it, and make a Collection called "Yellow" and add the chair to that as well.

To make a new Collection, click the "Add" button, and you'll be given a list of three types of Collections to choose from. The first two only apply when you are working with other people on the same project, and will be greyed out otherwise. The only other option is *Local Collection*.

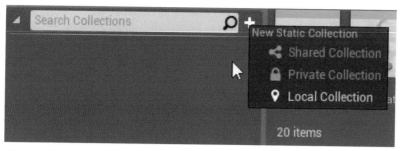

Figure 3.7.7 – Adding a new Collection

Directly to the left of the name of a Collection is an icon indicating what type of Collection it is. There is also a small box that will be grey when the Collection is empty and green when the Collection has content. To add an Asset to a Collection, simply click on the Asset and drag it onto the name of the Collection.

That's how to create *Static Collections*, but there's also a way to create what's called *Dynamic Collections*. For example, if you searched for "lamp" again in the Assets Window, and then clicked on the save icon to the right, you can save the search results as a Dynamic Collection. This doesn't save the Assets as the Collection, it saves the search query itself as the Collection. Meaning, every time you click on the "lamps" Collection, it will be performing that search and returning the results. So if a new Asset with the word "lamp" is added, that Asset would be automatically added to this Collection.

You can see which of your Collections are Static and which are Dynamic by looking at the icon to the right. A rectangular icon indicates a Static Collection, while a lightning icon indicates a Dynamic Collection.

Figure 3.7.8 – The icons to the right indicate if the Collection is Static or Dynamic

Thumbnail Options

The last group of options in the View Options menu concern the thumbnail images of the Assets. The slider is used to scale the size of the thumbnails larger or smaller.

The next option is *Thumbnail Edit Mode*. Clicking on this gives you the ability to change the perspective on the thumbnails. When you're in Thumbnail Edit Mode, there will be a yellow banner across the bottom, and when you click on a thumbnail and drag, instead of dragging that Asset, it will rotate the image of the Asset within the thumbnail. After you are finished, you can click "Done Editing" to exit Thumbnail Edit Mode.

The final option is *Real-Time Thumbnails*. Some Materials, such as a water Material, have an associated animation. Unchecking Real-Time Thumbnails will turn the animation off in the Content Browser. Note that the Material will still have that animation, the preview of that animation will simply be turned off in the thumbnail.

Content Browser Windows

If you ever close the Content Browser, you can quickly reopen it by going up to the Toolbar and clicking the Content button. This is useful if you want to keep the Content Browser closed while you are editing existing items in your Level, giving you a large Viewport to work with, but still have a way to quickly reopen it.

Figure 3.7.9 – The Content button will reopen the Content Browser

Also, the Unreal Editor allows you to have up to four Content Browsers open at once. If you go up to the file menu and go to Window > Content Browser, you can open up to three additional Content Browsers. If you have multiple monitors, you can drag these additional Content Browsers over to those monitors and work on them from there.

Another piece of functionality relating to multiple Content Browsers is the lock button in the upper-right. To understand the lock button, we must temporarily jump ahead a bit and introduce the Find button within the Details Panel.

For example, let's say a Static Mesh Actor is selected. Pressing the Find button in the Static Mesh category of the Details Panel will navigate the Content Browser directly to the Static Mesh Asset being used by that Actor. Clicking the Find button in the Materials category will navigate to the Material being used by that Actor.

Figure 3.7.10 – Clicking the Find button will navigate the Content Browser directly to that Asset

However, if you are in a certain folder in the Content Browser and want to remain in that folder, you can click the lock button to lock that Content Browser down, and now when you click on one of the Find buttons, it will open that Asset in a *new* Content Browser, instead of changing the location in the current one.

3.8 Details Panel

When you select an Actor, the Details Panel will display lots of information about that Actor, most of which is editable. At the top of the Details Panel is the name of the Actor, which can be changed.

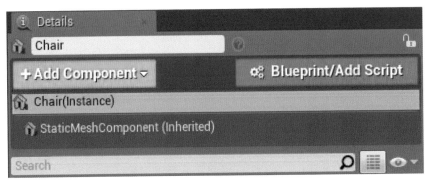

Figure 3.8.1 – The top of the Details Panel

To the right of that box you will see a Lock icon. By toggling the Lock icon to the locked setting, this will keep the details of the currently selected Actor locked in the Details Panel, even if other Actors are selected.

Below that is a button for adding a component to the Actor and a button for creating a Blueprint out of the Actor. Below that, you will see the component structure of the Actor. Components and Blueprints will be covered in detail in a later chapter.

Looking at the Details Panel, you will see that it is mostly comprised of properties of the selected Actor, and that those properties are grouped into Categories. This can be a long list, so there is a search box available to quickly find a property or category.

Property Matrix

To the right of the search box is a button that will launch the *Property Matrix*. The Property Matrix is for bulk comparison and editing of properties. Meaning it is used to compare and edit the values of properties of multiple Actors at once.

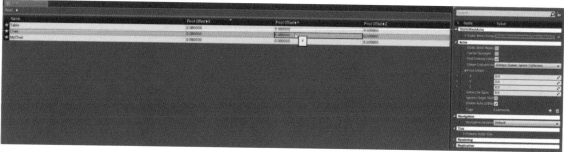

Figure 3.8.2 – The Property Matrix

Whichever Actors are selected when the button is pressed will be opened in the Property Matrix. By default, the Grid will start with just the Name column, which will display the name of the Actors that have been selected.

To the right of the Grid is a menu of properties that are common to all the selected Actors. This menu can be used to select which properties should be displayed as columns in the Grid. Just like with the Details Panel itself, there is a search bar you can use to search for a category or property.

To "pin" a property to the grid, click on the pin icon to the left of the name. This can be used to quickly compare lots of properties between Actors and quickly edit their values. You can sort by a column by clicking on the column label. You can edit the values by clicking in any of the cells and making changes. You can copy and paste values between cells, and so on.

View Options

To the right of the Property Matrix button is the View Options menu for the Details Panel.

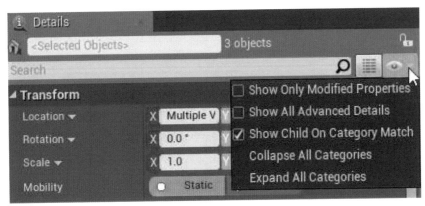

Figure 3.8.3 – View Options in the Details Panel

First on the list is *Show Only Modified Properties*. This will hide any properties that still have their default values and only show you those properties which have been modified since this Actor was created.

Next is *Show All Advanced Details*. At the bottom of some of the categories in the Details Panel, there is a little strip with a downward facing triangle in it. This means that the category has "Advanced Details." Advanced Details are properties that are less commonly used and are thus hidden by default to reduce clutter. To view Advanced Details for a category, you can simply click on the strip with the triangle to expand the menu, and then click it again to collapse it. But if you want to expand all of the Advanced Details menus at once, you could do so by checking Advanced Details in this menu here.

Next is *Show Child on Category Match*. This is checked by default, but when it is unchecked, the search bar will no longer try to match the text with Category names, it will only search the property names.

By default, all the categories in the Details Panel are expanded. However, they can be collapsed if you wish. You have the option to collapse or expand them individually by clicking on the triangle to the left of their names. But with the View Menu, you also have the option to collapse them all at once by clicking *Collapse All Categories* or expanding them all at once by clicking *Expand All Categories*.

Transform Category

The Details Panel has a lot of functionality in it that is specific to the type of Actor selected, but the Transform category is common to all Actors.

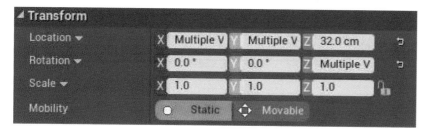

Figure 3.8.4 – The Transform Category of the Details Panel

Earlier, you learned how to transform Actors using the Move, Rotate, and Scale tools. But another way to move, rotate, and scale Actors is to use the Transform category of the Details Panel. The tools are useful when placement and scale don't need to be exact and you want to transform things quickly. But for finer precision or when exact values are needed, you can use the Details Panel to insert exact values manually.

The location of an Actor can be changed by changing the X, Y, and Z coordinates in the Location row. For Rotation, you can enter the number of degrees manually, or left-click on the arrows and drag left and right to adjust the value.

With Scale, you can directly enter a multiplier to scale by. For example, if the Z scale for a chair is currently 1.0, and you change it to 0.5, it will make the chair half as tall. But if you change it from 1.0 to 2.0 instead, it will double the height of the chair.

To the right of the Scale numbers, there is a little lock icon. When it is unlocked, and one of the numbers is changed, it affects that axis only. But let's say you want to scale an Actor uniformly, you can click on the lock icon to toggle it to locked, and now any change made to one of the axes will apply to them all equally.

Unless they are already set to their default values, each group of numbers will have a yellow arrow icon to their right. Clicking this icon will reset those numbers to their default values, which, for Location and Rotation is all zeroes, and for Scale is all ones.

When multiple Actors are selected, any values that happen to be common to all the Actors selected will be displayed, but in all other cases, the text "Multiple Values" will be displayed in the box instead. Entering a value in the box will apply that value to all Actors selected.

Relative vs World

By clicking on their labels, you can change the Location, Rotation, or Scale "type" to either *Relative* or *World*. So far, all the Actors we've worked with have had the world itself as its parent, so in those cases there is no difference between the two settings.

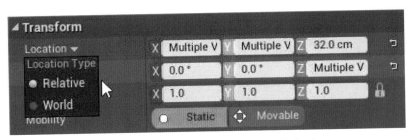

Figure 3.8.5 – Setting the Location Type to Relative

In Unreal, Actors can have parent Actors and/or child Actors. This concept will be discussed in more detail in the next section, but for now, just imagine that there is a cone Actor that is set to be the child of a chair Actor. Put another way, the chair is the parent of the cone.

If Location is set to Relative, and the coordinates of the cone are set to 0-0-0, the cone will be located directly in the center of the chair, its parent. But if Location is set to World, the cone will now be located at the center of the world, instead of at the center of its parent.

Mobility

Mobility is a setting that applies mainly to Static Mesh Actors and Light Actors.

For Static Meshes, there are two options - *Static* and *Moveable*. Static means that the Actor will remain stationary the entire time, while Moveable means that it is possible for the Actor's location to change. To clarify, the "static" in "Static Mesh" refers to the fact that the Mesh doesn't have any moving parts relative to itself, while the Static mobility setting means that the Actor's location will never change.

With Light Actors, there is a third option - *Stationary*. This is used for Lights that don't move, but can change in other ways such as being turned on or off, or having its color change.

So what's the point of the Mobility setting? Why not just make all Actors moveable even if they are just meant to be decorative? The answer is that moveable Actors require more processing power than static Actors because of things like light and shadow rendering. If an Actor is static, the Engine can predetermine how these things should look. So you should always make an Actor static if you can, and only increase the Mobility if you need it.

3.9 World Outliner

The *World Outliner* is used as an organized list of all the Actors in your Level. By default, it is located in the upper-right of the Level Editor.

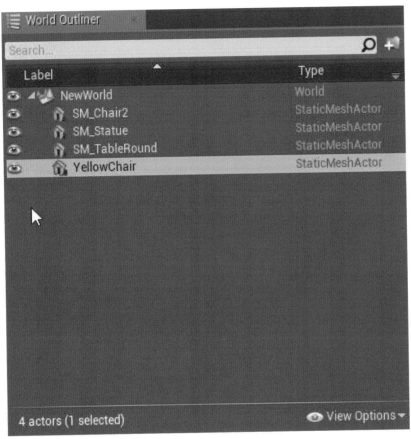

Figure 3.9.1 – The World Outliner

Clicking on one of the Actors in the World Outliner will select that Actor in the Viewport. Double-clicking will focus on that Actor in the Viewport. This is useful if you have a Level you've been working on for a long time and it has hundreds or even thousands of Actors and you want to go to a specific one. Instead of hunting for it visually throughout your Level, you can just find it in the World Outliner list, double-click, and it will take you straight to it.

World Outliner Data

The World Outliner is comprised of several individual columns. The main column contains the name of the Actor, which can be changed to whatever you like. There are a few ways you can do this. Just like with a file in Windows, if the Actor is already selected and is left-clicked again, it will allow you to rename it. You can also select the Actor and press *F2* to achieve the same result. Or, you can select the Actor, then come down to the box in the Details Panel and rename it from there.

In the left-most column is an icon of an eye for each row. This is a button that will toggle the visibility of the Actor on and off in the Viewport. This is useful when you are working on your Level and you have, for example, a large wall or some other Actor that is getting in the way and making it hard to see what you're doing; you can just toggle it's visibility off temporarily to make things easier.

The right-most column lists the type of the Actor. The icon directly to the left of the name of the Actor also gives this information. A small grey house icon is used for Static Mesh Actors and a blue box is used for Brush Actors, and so on. Each type of Actor will have their own special icon. This icon also displays other information. If an Actor's mobility is set to Moveable, an orange dot will appear on the icon. If it is set to Stationary, a yellow dot will appear. If it is set to Static, no dot will appear.

The Actors in the World Outliner can be listed alphabetically. Clicking at the top of the column with the Actors' names will sort the list alphabetically by name. Clicking again will sort the list in reverse alphabetical order. Clicking at the top of the Type column will sort the list alphabetically by type.

Grouping Actors

Another feature of the World Outliner is that you can use it to attach Actors to one another. Dragging the listing of one Actor onto the listing of another will make the first Actor a child of the second Actor. Children will be listed under their parents and indented to the right.

When you move a Parent, it will automatically move all of the Children of that Parent the same amount. But this doesn't work in reverse. Moving a Child will not affect its Parent.

If you want to manipulate a group of Actors all at once, but it doesn't make sense to make any parent-child relationships out of them, you just want them all grouped as equals, you can do that too. First, you need to select all the Actors you wish to be part of the Group. If you want to quickly select a long list of sequential Actors, you can select the first Actor then hold down the *Shift* key and press the down key to continually select the Actors below it. Or you can hold down the *Ctrl* key and left-click on each of the Actors you wish to select, or click on them again to deselect them.

If you have multiple Actors selected, you will still only see the Move/Rotate/Scale tool on one of them - the last one that was selected. But if you use the tool, it will still apply the same effect to all the Actors in the grouping.

To make a grouping "permanent," you can formally define a selection of Actors as a *Group* by pressing *Ctrl+G*. You will see green brackets around the Actors, letting you know that they are a Group. To ungroup Actors, press *Shift+G*. Alternatively, with your Actors selected, you can right-click on them, and select "Group" or "Ungroup" from the pop-up menu.

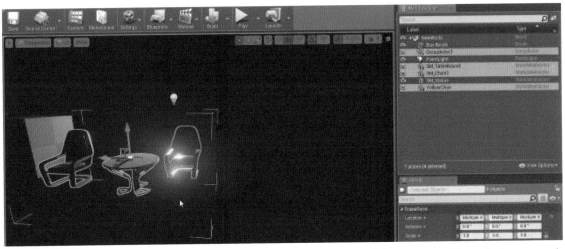

Figure 3.9.2 – Actors that have been defined as a Group will have green brackets around them

When you create a Group, this will also create a "Group Actor" in the World Outliner, which you can rename to your liking. To select the Group in the World Outliner, you can either select any of the Actors in the Group or just select the Group Actor itself.

So what if you've just done a lot of work grouping several Actors together and then decide you want to adjust one of the individual Actors within the Group? Luckily, there is a way to do this without having to ungroup the Actors and then selecting and grouping them all again. In this situation, you can temporarily "unlock" the Group, which will allow you to move, rotate, or scale the individual Actors without affecting the others, and then "lock" the Group again once you're finished.

All Groups are locked by default upon creation. A locked Group is indicated by the green brackets around them. To unlock a Group, right-click within the Group, scroll down to "Groups" in the menu, and select "Unlock." The brackets around the Group will turn to red, indicating that the Group is unlocked. Adjustments to the individual Actors within the Group can now be made. When you are done, right-click again, go down to "Groups" and select "Lock" to lock the Group once more.

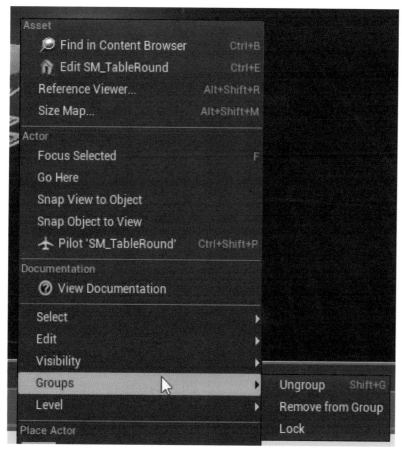

Figure 3.9.3 – Locking and unlocking Groups

Unlocking a Group does one other thing. It also allows you to remove individual Actors from a Group. With a Group unlocked, if you right-click on one of the individual Actors in the Group, and go down to Groups, there will be an option to "Remove from Group." If you click that, it will remove the Actor from the Group while still keeping all the other Actors grouped together.

Organizing and Finding Actors

As mentioned before, the main purpose of the World Outliner is to be able to organize and find your Actors. One way to help organize your Actors is by grouping them into folders. To create a new folder in the World Outliner, click on the New Folder icon, and it will create a new folder which can then be named. If you click on the New Folder icon while an Actor is selected, it will create the folder and then automatically add the Actor to that folder.

The World Outliner also has its own search bar. If you know the name of the Actor you're looking for, you can type it in the search bar and it will return all matches, even partial matches. For an exact match, meaning the query has to match the name exactly, put a plus sign in front of the search term. To exclude something from the search results, type the word preceded by a negative sign.

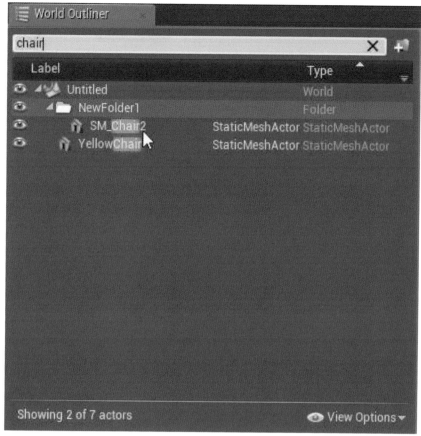

Figure 3.9.4 – Using the World Outliner to search for Actors

3.10 Chapter 3 Quiz

1. What is the difference between the Unreal Engine and the Unreal Editor?

2. What is the main editor of the Unreal Editor?

3. What is the window in the Level Editor called that gives you a visual representation of your Level?

4. What is the first mode of the Modes Panel?

5. What button or key, when held down, will cause you to rotate your view in the Viewport when the mouse is dragged and will also allow you to navigate the Viewport with WASD movement?

6. What button or key is used to focus on objects in the Viewport?

7. What three buttons or keys are used to select the Move, Rotate, and Scale Tools?

8. How do you use the Move Tool to make a copy of an Actor?

9. What button or key is used to snap an Actor to the nearest surface?

10. What button or key is used to enter and exit Immersive Mode (fullscreen)?

11. How can you hide all Actors and icons in the Viewport that won't be visible when the game is running?

12. In the Transform Category of the Details Panel, what is the lock icon to the right of the Scale values used for?

13. What does it mean when a Light Actor has a Mobility setting of Stationary?

14. True or False: Moving an Actor will also move that Actor's parent.

Answers

1. The Unreal Editor is the application used to *create* games and the Unreal Engine is the application that *runs* the games.

2. The Level Editor

3. Viewport

4. Place Mode

5. right mouse button

6. *F* key

7. *W, E,* and *R* keys

8. Hold down the *Alt* key and use the mouse to drag one of the Move Tool's three colored arrows.

9. *End* key

10. *F11* key

11. Press the *G* key to enter Game View.

12. Toggling the icon to a locked status will cause the selected Actor to scale uniformly when scaling any of the axes.

13. The Light can't change location but can change in other ways, such as being turned on or off, or having its color change.

14. False. Moving a parent will also move the child, but not vice-versa.

4

Actors

4.1 Static Meshes

A *mesh* is a 3D model of an object. There are two specific types of meshes that you can use as Actors in the Unreal Engine. These are the *Static Mesh* and the *Skeletal Mesh*.

A Static Mesh is a Mesh that doesn't bend, deform, or change shape in any way. A Static Mesh can still move around on the screen, it just can't animate. For example, you could use a Static Mesh in the shape of a cube to represent a cardboard box, and you could have that box slide across a surface, or fall off a table, or fly across the room, but you couldn't have flaps that open and close. For objects with moving parts, you would use a Skeletal Mesh.

There are a few different Static Mesh Actors in Place Mode of the Modes Panel. Under the Basic tab, there are Static Meshes in the shape of a cube, sphere, cylinder, and cone. These can be dragged into the Level, and then positioned, rotated, and scaled as desired.

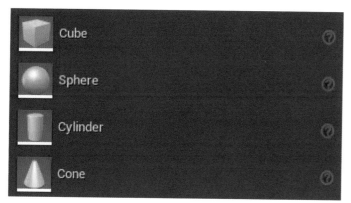

Figure 4.1.1 – The Modes Panel contains Static Meshes in the form of some basic shapes

While there are some basic Static Meshes in the Modes Panel, more often than not you will be dragging and dropping Static Meshes from the Content Browser that you import in. The Starter Content comes with some Static Meshes, but this is a small supply. You will want to import in meshes that you download or create yourself in a 3D-modeling application. The final chapter of this book will show you where you can download collections of meshes and other content for you to use in your games.

Replacing the Mesh of a Static Mesh Actor

In Unreal, the static mesh itself is actually a property of the Static Mesh Actor. For example, if you drag a mesh of a chair into the Level, Unreal will create a Static Mesh Actor and assign the chair mesh as the mesh to use for that Actor. You could then tell Unreal to use a mesh of a couch for that Actor and you would have a couch at the same location, rotation, and scale as the chair was.

One way to replace the mesh of an Actor is to use the dropdown in the Static Mesh category of the Details Panel. The dropdown will contain a search box you can use to find the mesh you want to use.

Figure 4.1.2 – You can use the dropdown in the Static Mesh category to replace the mesh Asset that is used

Another way is to browse to the replacement mesh in the Content Browser, select it, and then click on the arrow in the Static Mesh category of the Details Panel. The arrow will replace the current mesh with whatever is selected in the Content Browser when you click it.

Physics

If you drag a Cube Mesh into a Level, and then press Play, the cube won't fall to the ground, it will just sit suspended in the air. If you press up against it, it won't move.

There are two reasons for this. The first reason is that the default Mobility of a Static Mesh Actor is Static. When the Mobility is Static, we are telling the engine that this Actor will never change its position or rotation for any reason. The Mobility will need to be set to Moveable before the cube will be able to move.

The second reason is that Static Meshes have physics turned off by default. To turn on physics for an Actor, with the Actor selected, go to the Physics category in the Details Panel and check the box next to *Simulate Physics*.

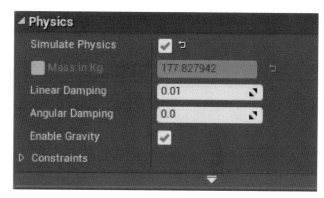

Figure 4.1.3 – The Physics category in the Details Panel

If you were to press Play after changing these two settings, the cube would now fall to the ground and you would be able to push it along the ground.

The Physics category has several other properties. One of them is the mass of the Actor, measured in kilograms. If you change the size of the Actor, it will increase or decrease its mass accordingly. Objects with more mass require more force applied against them in order to be affected. You can also set the mass directly without changing the size, which also has the effect of changing the density of the Actor.

The next two properties are *Linear Damping* and *Angular Damping*. Damping refers to the amount of drag that is applied to the movement of the object. Similar to having more mass, the more drag an Actor has, the harder it is to move. But in this case, drag is meant to represent friction on the object. For example, if a cube were a smooth block of ice, it would have less drag on it than a rough block of stone, even if the two had the same mass.

The *Linear Damping* property affects translational movement of the object, meaning a change in location, while the *Angular Damping* property affects rotational movement of the object, meaning a change in rotation. By increasing Linear Damping, an Actor won't travel as far when pushed, but will still spin just as easily. Decreasing the Linear Damping to a negative value will cause the Actor to travel farther when pushed, and still doesn't affect the spin. Increasing or decreasing the Angular Damping won't affect how far the Actor travels in response to force, but will make it easier or harder to spin the object.

Below the Angular Damping property is the *Enable Gravity* setting. If this is turned off, but Simulate Physics is on, an Actor will still react to force, but gravity will not affect it. This can replicate zero-gravity environments such as outer space.

4.2 Brushes

In the world of 3D modeling, a Brush is simply a 3D area of space. This is nearly identical to our understanding of what a Mesh is, but there are several key differences between Brushes and Meshes.

Brushes vs Meshes

The first difference is that Brushes are used for more basic shapes. In the Modes Panel, in the *BSP* tab, you can see the Brushes that are available. There are some basic geometric shapes and some Brushes in the shape of stairs. In the Basic tab, we also have some Static Meshes available in the form of basic geometric shapes, but Meshes can be much more complex than this, taking the form of furniture, cars, people, etc.

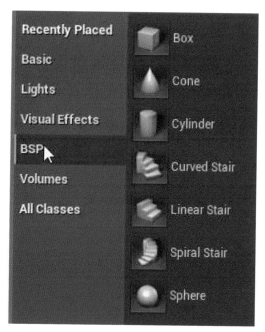

Figure 4.2.1 – The Brushes available in the BSP tab of Place Mode

The second key difference is in how the Unreal Engine handles Brushes and Meshes in memory. For example, let's say you make several copies of a Brush Actor. Each copy made gets stored in memory, and thus each copy made increases the memory demands of the game. However, no matter how many copies of a Mesh you make, it will not increase the memory needed at all. This is because a single Mesh only gets stored in memory once, no matter how many instances of it there are in your Level.

So Meshes look better and they perform better, but the advantage of Brushes is that they are easier to edit than the more complex Meshes. This makes Brushes better suited for making a prototype, or a rough draft, of a Level. So you can use Brushes to sculpt the basic layout of your Level and then replace those Brushes with Meshes once the layout is finalized. In theory, once you have the basic layout sculpted in Brushes, you won't need to keep making minor changes over and over to the more difficult to edit Meshes. While the final version of most games will have very little or no Brushes in it at all, chances are, each of its Levels started out made almost exclusively as Brushes.

Brush Settings

Brushes have several different properties available for you to edit under the Brush Settings category of the Details Panel.

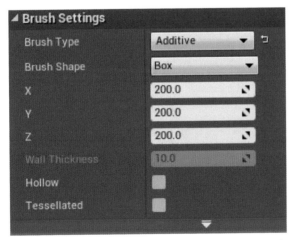

Figure 4.2.2 – Brush Settings for a Box Brush

Brush Type

Some of these properties are different, depending on the base shape of the Actor, but one property that is common to all Brushes is *Brush Type*. The Brush Type for any Brush can either be Additive or Subtractive. You can choose what type you want your Brush to be, before you drag it in, by choosing the type in the Modes Panel. Or you can change the type of an existing Brush, by changing it in the Details Panel.

The Additive type is pretty straight forward. An "additive" Brush will add geometry to the Level. A subtractive Brush, on the other hand, will subtract from existing geometry in the Level. For example, if a subtractive Cylinder Brush is dragged onto an additive Box Brush, wherever the subtractive Cylinder Brush is overlapping is causing the geometry that was there to be removed. You can think of subtractive Brushes as "holes" in the shape of the Brush.

This feature is one of the main reasons why Brushes are so well-suited to sculpting overall Level design. By adding and subtracting geometry in this way, you can sculpt the layout of a Level much faster than you could trying to use Meshes.

Brush Shape

The next property under Brush Settings is *Brush Shape*. Brush Shape simply refers to if the Brush is in the shape of a box, a cylinder, a cone, and so on. You can choose which Brush Shape to use by choosing which Actor to drag into the Level, but you can also change the shape of an existing Brush Actor in the Brush Settings category.

Size Properties

Some of the properties in Brush Settings are dependent on the shape of the Brush being used. For example, a Box Brush will have *X*, *Y*, and *Z* properties denoting the length of the Box in those dimensions. Adjusting these values will adjust the size of the Box. This is similar to using the Scale property in the Transform category, with one key difference when it comes to Materials that I will talk about in the section on Materials.

The Cylinder and Cone Brushes have their size determined by just a *Z* length, and an *Outer Radius* property. The Z is how tall the cone or cylinder is, and the Outer Radius is how wide around it is. For the Cone, this is the radius as measured at the base. For the Sphere Brush, radius is the only property used to determine its size.

Sides Properties

The Cylinder and Cone Brushes also have a property called *Sides*. As you might have noticed already with these Brush shapes, their "curved" edges, so to speak, aren't actually curves, but are made up of a series of flat sides. The Sides property determines how many of these flat sides the Brush has. The more sides it has, the smoother around it will appear.

The Sphere Brush has a property similar to this, which is the *Tessellation* factor. The higher this number is, the more sides the sphere will have, and the smoother it will appear.

The Cylinder and Cone Brushes also have the property *Align to Side*. If this is checked, it will align the sides of the Brush with the grid.

Hollow Property

Another property of Brushes that is common to the Box, Cone, and Cylinder Brush, is whether or not the Brush is *Hollow*. This is just what it sounds like. If this property is checked, instead of the Brush being solid all the way through, it will be hollow inside, and the Brush will essentially be a shell, with walls of some thickness. For Box Brushes, this is set with the *Wall Thickness* property. For Cylinder Brushes, this is set by the *Inner Radius* property. The Inner Radius is the radius of the hollow part. For Cone Brushes, this is set by both the Inner Radius property and the *Cap Z* property. The Cap Z property determines how tall the hollow area is within the cone. For each of these, the property is greyed out unless the Hollow property is checked.

One thing the Hollow feature is particularly useful for, is for quickly creating rooms or buildings. This can be done by making a large Box Brush, setting it to Hollow, and then using a smaller, subtractive Box Brush to make a doorway.

Stair Brushes

The *Linear Stair* is the simplest of the three Stair Brushes. It has Length, Height, and Width properties to determine the size of each individual step. You can also choose the number of steps for the staircase. The default is 10 but you can make this larger or smaller as you wish.

Figure 4.2.3 – A Linear Stair Brush

The *Add to First Step* property is essentially a Step Height property for the first step only. While the Step Height property increase or decreases the height of all of the steps, the Add to First Step property will only affect the height of the first step.

Brush Settings		
Brush Type	Additive	▼
Brush Shape	Linear Stair	▼
Step Length	30	
Step Height	20	
Step Width	200	
Num Steps	10	
Add to First Step	0	

Figure 4.2.4 – Brush Settings for a Linear Stair

The *Curved Stair* has some of the same properties as the Linear Stair, such as Step Height, Step Width, Number of Steps, and Add to First Step. But it also has some other properties as well that pertains to its curve.

Figure 4.2.5 – A Curved Stair Brush

The first of these properties is the *Inner Radius*. Imagine the Curved Stair wrapping around an invisible column. When the Curved Stair is selected, you will see the Transform tool at the center of this invisible column. The Inner Radius property sets the length between the center of this invisible column, and the edge of the staircase. In other words, it affects the width of this "invisible column."

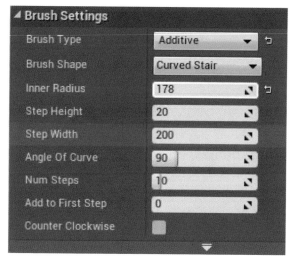

Figure 4.2.6 – Brush Settings for a Curved Stair

Next, is the *Angle of Curve* property. This will set the angle that is made between the two vectors pointing from the center of the invisible column to each end of the staircase. The default is 90 degrees.

Last, is the *Counter Clockwise* property. This one is pretty straightforward. With this unchecked, the staircase will curve in a clockwise direction. With it checked, the staircase will instead curve in a counter-clockwise direction.

The final staircase is the *Spiral Stair*. With the Spiral Stair, the Step Height property is a little different than it is on the other two stairs. With the Spiral Stair, the Step Height won't affect how tall each step is, it will affect how much each step overlaps the step above and below it.

Figure 4.2.7 – A Spiral Stair Brush

At the Default Value, each step overlaps its adjacent steps by about 50%. But if the value is increased, the amount of overlap will begin to decrease, and eventually the steps will no longer overlap and begin to have some distance from each other. If you want to make each step actually taller, you need to use the *Step Thickness*.

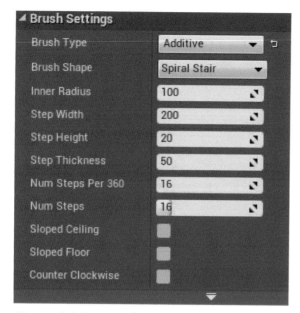

Figure 4.2.8 – Brush Settings for a Spiral Stair

The Spiral Staircase has a *Num Steps* property like the other two, but it also has a *Num Steps Per 360* property. This defines the number of steps in one full spiral of the staircase.

The next property is the *Sloped Ceiling* property. With this unchecked, the underside of the staircase will just resemble upside down stairs. If it is checked, it will make the underside completely smooth. With the *Sloped Floor* property, you can change the top surface of the staircase to be perfectly smooth. You can, in essence, change a staircase into a curved ramp.

4.3 Materials

In the Unreal Engine, a *Material* is an Asset that you can apply to the surface of a Brush or Mesh, to make that surface, and thus the geometry behind that surface, look like it's made out of a certain substance. For example, you could resize a Box Brush and use it as a wall. Then, if you apply a wood Material to the wall, it will look like a wooden wall.

Note that, while this chapter is focusing on the different Actor types, Materials aren't Actors themselves. They are simply an important property of Mesh and Brush Actors which is why they are being discussed here.

To apply a Material to a surface, select the Material in the Content Browser and drag it into the Viewport and onto the surface you wish to apply it to.

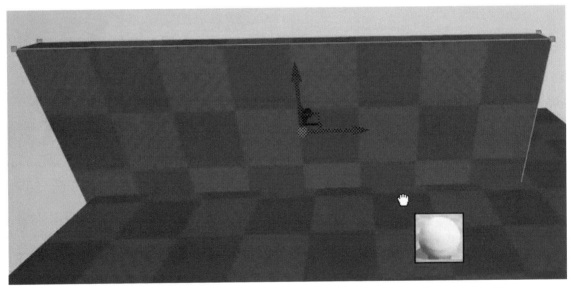

Figure 4.3.1 – Drag a Material onto a surface to apply it to the surface

Apply Material to All Surfaces

If you want a Material to be applied to all the surfaces of a Brush, one way to do this is to select the Material first, and with that Material selected in the Content Browser, drag the Brush Actor into the Level, and it will get created with that Material applied to all the surfaces of the Brush.

If you want to apply a Material to all the surfaces of a Brush that is already existing in your Level, perform the following steps:

1. Make sure you don't already have the Brush selected. If you do, just click on one of the other Actors in the World Outliner.

2. With the Brush unselected, click on one of the surfaces of the Brush to select just that surface. When only a surface or surfaces of the Brush is selected, and not the Brush itself, the *Surface Materials*, *Geometry*, and *Surface Properties* categories will appear in the Details Panel.

3. Go down to the Geometry category and click on "Select," then "Select All Adjacent Surfaces," or use the shortcut *Shift+J*, and now all the surfaces of the Brush will be selected.

4. Drag a Material onto the Brush and it will apply that Material to all the surfaces.

Surface Materials Category

In addition to dragging and dropping, another way you can apply a Material to a surface is to use the *Surface Materials* category of the Details Panel. This works just like replacing the Static Mesh did in the earlier section.

Figure 4.3.2 – The Surface Materials category

You can use the dropdown box to select the Material you want to use. Or you can select the Material you want to use in the Content Browser and then click on the arrow to apply it. Or, if you want to find the Material that is currently applied in the Content Browser, click on the magnifying glass to go straight to it.

Elements

A single Mesh can have different Materials applied to different parts of it. When a mesh gets created in a 3D-modeling program, such as Maya or 3D Studio Max, if it has different materials applied to different parts of its surface, once that mesh gets imported into the Unreal Editor, each of those sections of surface become known as Elements, and you will have the ability to apply a different Material to each Element.

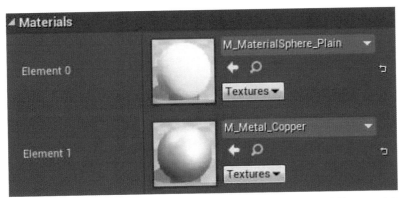

Figure 4.3.3 – Each Element of a Mesh can have a different Material

If you drag a Material onto the Mesh through the Viewport, the Material will only be applied to the specific Element it was dragged onto. In the Details Panel, in the Materials category, there will be one Element for each Material, and you can set them each individually.

Textures

We won't go into too much detail about *Textures* in this beginner-level book, but just know that Textures are what Materials are made of. A Material is made up of one or more Textures, and each Texture is just an image file that defines one of the properties of the Material. So one Texture may be the actual colors of the Material, while another Texture maps its smoothness or roughness, and so on. This data is combined to form the composite Material.

The Textures dropdown in the Materials category of the Details Panel will show you the Textures that make up the currently applied Material. If you select one, it will take you to that Texture in the Content Browser.

Surface Properties Category

When a Material is applied to the surface of a Brush, and you select that surface, there will be a *Surface Properties* category in the Details Panel. Before we discuss that, however, you need to understand how the axes of a Material are labeled. A Material is a 2-dimensional object, and normally you would use X and Y as the names of the axes of a 2D object. However, X and Y are already being used to describe two of the axes of our Levels. To avoid confusion, the letters U and V are used for the axes of a Material.

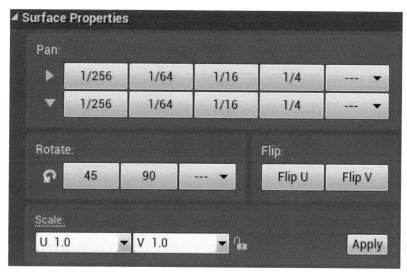

Figure 4.3.4 – The Surface Properties category

At the top of the Surface Properties category is a section where you can pan the Material across the surface of the object. The first row of buttons is used to pan the Material along its U-axis. The different values represent how much to pan with each click. The last column can be used to enter a custom amount. The second row of buttons is used to pan the Material along the V-axis.

Below that is a section where you can rotate the Material relative to the surface it's on. You can toggle which direction the Material will rotate, either clockwise or counterclockwise, and then there are buttons to rotate it 45 degrees, 90 degrees, or a custom amount.

To the right of that is a section where you can flip the Material, either along the U-axis or the V-axis.

Material Scaling

When you scale an Actor, the Material that is applied to it will get scaled as well, meaning it will get stretched or compressed. Even if you scale the Actor first, and then apply the Material, the effect will be the same.

With Static Meshes, there's no way around this. Brushes, however, are a bit more flexible. If the Material on a Brush surfaces gets scaled, you can see it in the Details Panel, in the Scale section of the Surface Properties category. To reset the scaling, you simply need to set the Scale property back to a 1:1 ratio, and then click the Apply button.

With Brushes, you can edit the dimensions directly, instead of having to rely on scaling. When you change the size of a Brush in this way, it doesn't change the scale ratio of the Material. So if you use the X, Y, and Z properties of the Brush, under the Brush Settings category, to change the size of the Brush, no matter what size you make the Brush, the ratio will remain 1:1.

4.4 Lights

In Unreal Engine, a *Light* is simply an Actor that will generate light for your Level. They are not meant to represent the object producing the light, only the light itself. You would use a Mesh for, say, a lamp or a flashlight and then use a Light Actor to produce the light itself.

Overview of Light Types

There are four types of Light Actors in Unreal. The first of these is the *Directional Light Actor*. The Directional Light Actor is used to emulate light coming from an extremely long distance away, such as outer space. All the light will hit the level at the same angle, meaning all shadows produced by this light will be parallel. This Actor is used primarily for sunlight and moonlight.

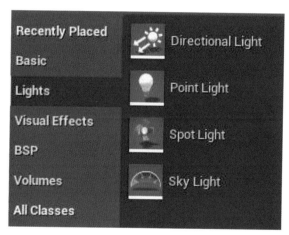

Figure 4.4.1 – The four Light Actors available in Unreal

Next is the *Point Light*. The Point Light will produce light that emanates in all directions. This is useful for mimicking the light coming from a light bulb, or fire, for example.

The *Spot Light*, on the other hand, will emit light in the shape of a cone. This is like the light coming from a flashlight, or, as the name suggests, a spot light, like they use at the theatre.

The *Sky Light Actor* is used to emulate the light that gets reflected off of the atmosphere, and other distant objects. When light comes from the sun or moon, a lot of it comes through as direct sunlight or moonlight. That's what the Directional Light Actor mentioned above represents. But some of that sunlight or moonlight hits particles in the atmosphere, or clouds, or distant mountaintops, and then gets reflected off those objects at a different angle. The Sky Light Actor represents that light that gets scattered in the atmosphere, or reflected off of other objects, and that comes through as weaker, indirect sunlight or moonlight at all different angles. In simpler terms, you could say it represents the faint glow of the atmosphere.

Building the Lighting

Changes to a Level will not affect the lighting like they should until the Editor is told to *build* the lighting.

Building the lighting just means that the Engine runs a lot of calculations to determine how the light and shadows should now look on objects based on the changes that have occurred since the last time the lighting was built.

To build the lighting, simply go up to the Toolbar and click on the Build button. The reason the Editor has you do this manually is because when you start to have many Actors and/or Lights in your Level, the build can take quite a while to perform. So, even if it only took ten seconds, you wouldn't want to have to wait those ten seconds every time you moved an Actor in your Level. This allows you to build only when you're ready.

Figure 4.4.2 – The Build button

Directional Light

The *Directional Light* is used to represent sunlight or moonlight. It has several properties that can be viewed and edited in the Details Panel.

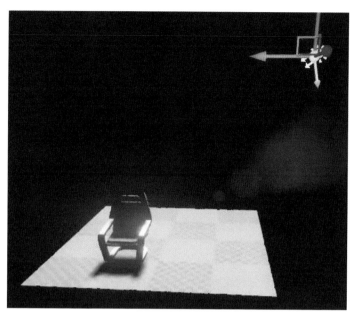

Figure 4.4.3 – A Directional Light Actor

One of these properties is the Light's Mobility. If a Light is Static, that means that not only can it not move, it can't change color, or brightness, or any other property while the game is running. If a Light is Stationary, it still can't move, but it can change its color, brightness, or other properties during the game. If a Light is Moveable, it can move and change its other properties during the game. As you move to the right along these three settings, they get more flexible in terms of what the Light can do, but they also demand more resources from the processor.

Intensity

In the Light category of the Details Panel, there are several more properties of the Light that can be edited. The first of these properties is *Intensity*. This controls the brightness of the Light. Increasing the Intensity makes the Light get brighter and decreasing the Intensity makes the Light get dimmer.

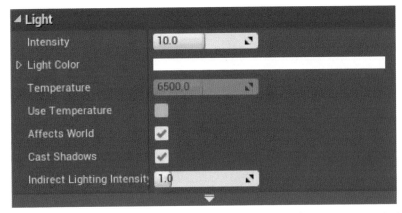

Figure 4.4.4 – The Light category properties of a Directional Light

Light Color

The next property is the *Light Color*. By default, the color of a Light is white, but this can be changed. There are two ways to change the Light Color property. One way is to click on the triangle to the left of the property name and expand the RGB menu. With the RGB menu, you can adjust the amount of red, green, and blue in the Light to determine its overall color.

The second way to edit the Light Color is to click on the strip, to the right of the property name, that previews the color. This will open the *Color Picker*. The Color Picker is available in several places in the Unreal Editor where there is a need to select a color.

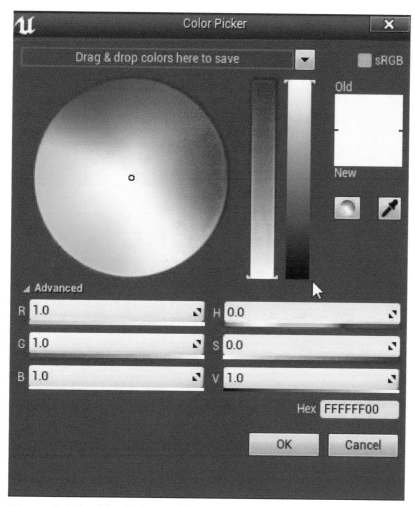

Figure 4.4.5 – The Color Picker

The Color Picker actually gives you several ways in which you can select a color. You can select one from the color wheel. You can adjust the saturation and the brightness using a pair of sliders. You can set the Hue, Saturation, and Brightness values directly. It is another place where you can set the Red, Green, and Blue values. And finally, you can use the hexadecimal representation of a color if you wish.

Temperature

The next two properties relate to the *Temperature* of the Light. Temperature changes the color of the Light based on how hot you tell the Engine the light source is supposed to be. By default, Temperature is not used, but if you want to use it, you can check the *Use Temperature* property.

If you've ever looked at the fire in a fireplace, for example, you will notice it's made up of different colors. Most of it is red, but as you go inwards, it starts to get more orange, and then you may see wisps of purple and blue. The bluish parts are actually the hottest parts of the fire. So as the Temperature setting is decreased, the Light will shine redder, and as it is increased, the Light will shine bluer.

Affects World

The next property is *Affects World*. This simply toggles whether the Light is enabled or disabled. If this is unchecked, it will be as if the Light isn't even in the Level.

Cast Shadows

The next property is *Cast Shadows*, which determines if the Light will cause shadows to be cast when objects block the Light's path. You would want this checked for a more realistic environment. However, shadows are processor-intensive, so if you were in need of performance savings you might choose to uncheck this for some of the Lights in your Level.

Indirect Lighting Intensity

The last property in the Light category is *Indirect Lighting Intensity*. If some light gets reflected off of another surface, that reflected light is called "indirect lighting" and can also light up objects in the Level. This property will determine how much this reflected light affects the other objects it shines upon.

Point Light

The *Point Light* emanates light in all directions. It has many of the same properties that the Directional Light has, with a few additional ones as well.

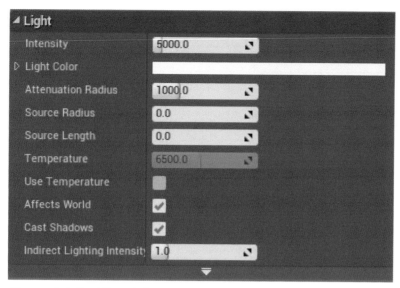

Figure 4.4.6 – The Light category properties of a Point Light

The first of these is the *Attenuation Radius*. This determines how far from the source the Light will still affect objects in your Level. In the Level Editor, this is represented by a blue sphere. The higher the Attenuation Radius, the larger the sphere will be, and the farther the light will extend from its source.

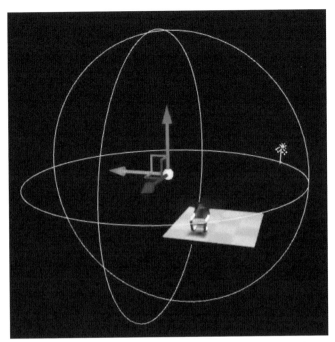

Figure 4.4.7 – The attenuation sphere surrounding a Point Light

The next two properties are *Source Radius* and *Source Length*. The light from a Point Light will actually emanate from a single point in the Level. However, let's say you have a Light that is supposed to be coming from a long, thin fluorescent bulb, and it is above a very shiny floor. If there were a reflection of the bulb in the floor, you would want it to be in the same shape as the bulb. So you can use the Source Radius and Source Length properties to adjust the size and shape that the light source will appear in reflections.

Spot Light

The *Spot Light* is very similar to the Point Light, except that instead of shining light in all directions, it shines it in a specific direction, in a cone shape. The Spot Light has all the same properties as the Point Light, with the addition of two more properties - the *Inner Cone Angle* and the *Outer Cone Angle*.

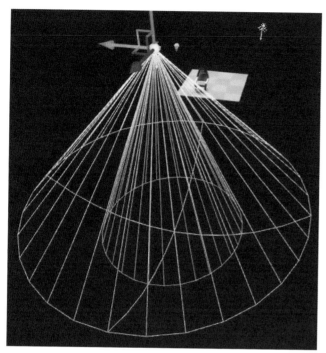

Figure 4.4.8 – A Spot Light Actor

Within the Inner Cone of the Spot Light, the light will be at its brightest and will be just as bright at any spot within the Inner Cone. From the outer edge of the Inner Cone to the outer edge of the Outer Cone, the Intensity of the light will gradually fall off to nothing.

So you can use the Inner Cone Angle and the Outer Cone Angle to set the size of these cones and determine how much of the light is at full brightness and how much of the light is part of the gradual falloff portion.

Sky Light

The *Sky Light* is used to represent the reflection of light from the atmosphere or far away objects in the sky such as clouds or mountaintops. To determine at what distance this Light should appear to emanate from, we need to define at what distance the sky should be considered to start at.

Figure 4.4.9 – A Sky Light Actor

By default, the Sky Light's *Source Type* property will be set to "SLS Captured Scene," which just means that the sky will be defined as any point that is the *Sky Distance Threshold* away from the Sky Light Actor. So if the Sky Light is placed at the center of the Level, with a Sky Distance Threshold of 150,000, you are saying that the sky should begin 150,000 units from the center of the Level.

There is also the option to change the Source Type to "SLS Specified Cubemap," and then provide a file called a Cubemap to define the area that should be considered the sky. However, Cubemaps are beyond the scope of this beginner-level book and won't be covered.

4.5 Atmospheric Fog

The *Atmospheric Fog Actor* is used to add a realistic looking atmosphere to a Level. The Atmospheric Fog Actor can be found in the Visual Effects tab in Place Mode of the Modes Panel.

The Directional Light Actor can be used to represent sunlight, but this alone won't make the Level look like it's outside. Atmospheric Fog will add a blue sky and a sun disc, and will cause objects to get a little foggy when they are far away in the distance.

Figure 4.5.1 – The Atmospheric Fog Actor adds an atmosphere to the Level

Sun Disc

By default, the sun disc of the Atmospheric Fog will appear on the horizon, giving a look of sunrise or sunset. But it is possible to combine the Atmospheric Fog Actor with the Directional Light Actor, which will cause the sun to appear in the sky. To do so, check the property *Atmosphere Sun Light* of the Directional Light Actor. This property can be found in the Light category.

Figure 4.5.2 – Here, the Engine is using the rotation of the Directional Light to determine where to place the sun disc in the sky

If the Atmosphere Sun Light property is checked, the Atmospheric Fog will use the rotation of the Directional Light to determine where the sun disc should be placed in the sky. The Engine will look at the direction that the light rays from the Directional Light are set to hit the Level, and then calculate where in the sky the Sun should be for that to make sense. If you use the Rotation Tool on the Directional Light to change the angle of the light rays, it will change the location of the sun disc in the sky.

Atmospheric Fog Properties

The first property under the Atmosphere category is *Sun Multiplier*. The higher its value, the brighter the sky and the fog will appear. In other words, you can use it to make the Level look more or less sunny.

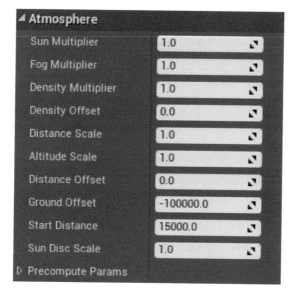

Figure 4.5.3 – The properties of an Atmospheric Fog Actor

The next three properties affect the fog only. They are also somewhat subtle in their effects, especially when the fog is far away. The *Fog Multiplier* property affects how much the light affects the fog. Higher values will make the fog seem brighter. The *Density Multiplier* affects how dense the fog is. Higher values will make the fog denser and lower values will make it less dense. The *Density Offset* affects the opacity of the fog. Higher values will make the fog more opaque, while lower values will make the fog more transparent. Basically, these three properties will make the fog seem more or less thick in subtly different ways.

The next property is *Distance Scale*. This will affect the scale of the units of any other properties of the Actor that have to do with distance. For example, changing the Distance Scale from 1 to 2 will cause any distance units to be double in length. Setting the Distance Scale higher is useful when you have a large Level and it would be easier to work with larger units of distance.

The *Altitude Scale* is just like the Distance Scale except it only affects the Z-axis, whereas the Distance Scale affects all three dimensions.

Next, is the *Ground Offset* property. This tells the Engine where sea level should be considered to be at in our Level. This is important to the Atmospheric Fog Actor, as the fog will only appear at places above sea level. The default value is -100,000. This is saying that sea level starts at -100,000 on the Z-axis. So if the ground of our Level is placed at 0 on the Z-axis, this means that our Level is 100,000 centimeters, or 1000 meters, above sea level.

The *Start Distance* property controls how far away from the camera the Level will start to appear foggy. Higher values will make the fog appear distant and lower values will make the fog appear close.

The *Sun Disc Scale* property is very straightforward. It simply defines the size of the sun disc. Increasing its value will make the sun appear bigger in the sky and decreasing its value will make the sun appear smaller.

Figure 4.5.4 – Setting the Sun Disc Scale to a high value will make the sun appear large in the sky

4.6 Player Start Actor

If a Level does not contain a *Player Start Actor*, the player will begin the Level at position (0,0,0). If you want to have control over where the player will start the Level, you need to place a Player Start Actor.

The Player Start Actor can be accessed from the Modes Panel under the Basic tab. Wherever you place it is where the player will start when the Level begins. It can also be used to specify the direction the player should be facing when the Level starts. The light blue arrow coming out of the Actor indicates the direction. You can rotate the Actor to change the direction the arrow is pointing.

Figure 4.6.1 – The Player Start Actor

If you ever place your Player Start Actor somewhere in the Level where it intersects with another object, the icon of the game controller will change to a label that says "Bad Size". To make sure the player doesn't start the Level stuck in something, move the Player Start Actor to a position where the icon shows the controller instead.

Figure 4.6.2 – If the Player Start Actor intersects with another object, it will display a "Bad Size" label

While you are developing your Levels, you will often want to test something or look at something in-game right in the spot you are at in the Viewport at that moment instead of wherever the Player Start Actor might be. To do so, right-click in the Viewport, and then choose *Play From Here* towards the bottom of the menu.

If you want to move around the Viewport and continually start the Level at wherever you are at that moment, you can go to the drop-down menu to the right of the Play button and choose to *Spawn Player At… > Current Camera Location*. When you want to go back to using the Player Start Actor, go back to the drop-down menu and choose to Spawn Player At… > *Default Player Start*.

4.7 Components

Components are various objects or functionality that can be attached to Actors. There are many different kinds of Components. Some of the types of Components are objects that are also used as Actors on their own. For example, you could attach a Static Mesh as a Component to another Actor. Or, you could attach a Light as a Component to another Actor.

Other Components, such as *Movement Components*, do not have their own Actor type and are only used as Components on other Actors. For example, a *Rotating Movement Component* attached to an Actor will cause that Actor to rotate, but doesn't have any use on its own.

Adding Components

When you want to attach a Component to an Actor, select that Actor, then go over to the Details Panel and click on the green button that says *Add Component*. You'll get a long list of different Components you can add, grouped by category. There will also be a search bar that you can use to quickly find a type of Component by name.

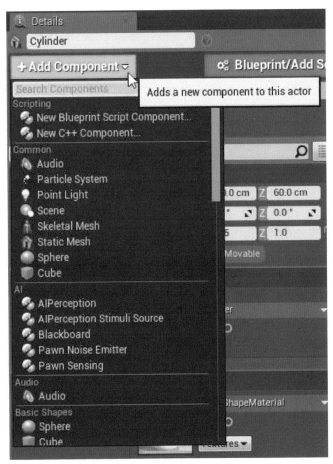

Figure 4.7.1 – Use the Add Component button in the Details Panel to add a component to an Actor

To add a Static Mesh from the Content Browser as a Component, after clicking on Add Component, instead of choosing one of the pre-made meshes available in the Modes Panel, click on the generic "Static Mesh." This will add an empty Static Mesh Component to the Actor. You can then choose which Static Mesh to use by using the Static Mesh section of the Details Panel.

Component Structure

Below the Add Component button is a section where you can see the Component structure of an Actor. There is a parent-child relationship where Components can have sub-Components which, in turn, can have their own sub-Components. Sub-components will appear underneath their parent Components and will be indented further to the right than their parent. If you move or rotate a Component, it will move or rotate all of its sub-Components as well.

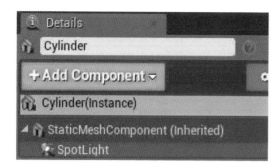

Figure 4.7.2 – The Component structure of an Actor. Here, a Spot Light is a child of a Static Mesh Component, which is a child of a Cylinder Mesh.

Rotating Movement Component

A *Rotating Movement Component* will cause the Actor it is attached to, to rotate. It can be added by clicking "Add Component," going down to the "Movement" category, and selecting "Rotating Movement." If the Mobility setting of the Actor has been set to Moveable, it will begin to spin around as soon as the Level begins.

The Rotating Movement Component has some properties you can edit. The first property is *Rotation Rate*, which specifies how much to rotate the Actor and in which direction. Whatever angle you enter, it will rotate the Actor that many degrees per second. For example, setting the Yaw rotation, which means rotation around the Z-axis, to 180 degrees will cause the Actor to spin one full 360-degree rotation, in that direction, every two seconds.

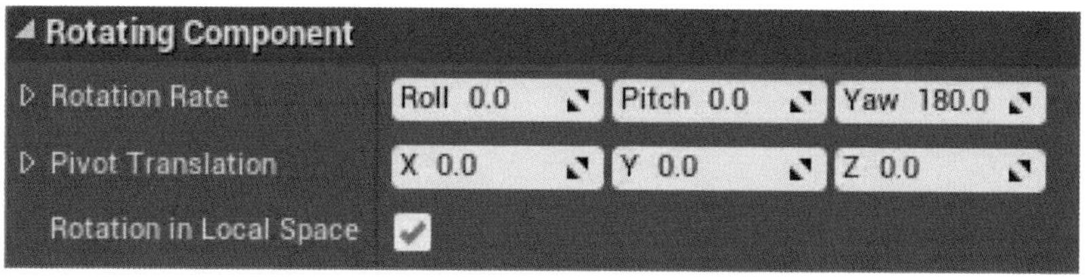

Figure 4.7.3 – The properties of a Rotating Movement Component

Another property you can edit is the *Pivot Translation*. By default, with this at (0,0,0), the Actor will rotate around its center. However, you can enter X, Y, and Z values to change the pivot point to a different location. For example, a value of 100 for the X-value will cause the Actor to rotate around a point 100 units, along the X-axis, from the center of the Actor.

4.8 Volumes

In the Unreal Engine, a *Volume* is a 3D area of space that is invisible to the player and serves a specific purpose depending on its type. A Volume is actually another type of Brush. However, for the remainder of this book, Volume Brushes will be referred to as simply Volumes in order to avoid confusion with Geometry Brushes.

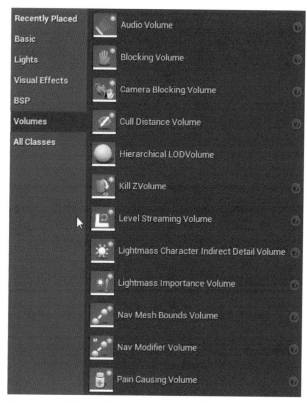

Figure 4.8.1 – There are several Volumes available in the Volumes tab of Place Mode

Blocking Volumes

You can access a variety of Volumes from the Volumes tab in the Modes Panel. For example, a *Blocking Volume* will prevent Actors from being able to enter that Volume. So you can use them as a type of force field, or just to block off areas of your Level where you don't intend for players to go.

A *Camera Blocking Volume* is just like a Blocking Volume except it only blocks Cameras. This is useful in third-person games when you want to keep the Camera confined to certain parts of the Level.

Trigger Volumes

Perhaps the most important type of Volume is the *Trigger Volume*. Trigger Volumes are used to trigger something called an *Event* when an Actor enters or exits them. In the next chapter, *Blueprints*, you will learn how to define a set of instructions for the Engine to perform when certain Events occur.

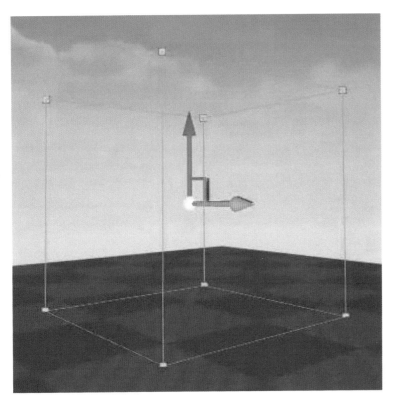

Figure 4.8.2 – A Trigger Volume

For example, if you had a haunted house in your Level, you could place a Trigger Volume in the doorway of the entrance, and name it "PlayerEntersHouseVolume." Then, using a Blueprint, you would be able to define an Event, and name it something like

"PlayerEntersHouseEvent," that should fire off a set of instructions any time the player enters the PlayerEntersHouseVolume.

Those instructions could be anything you want, such as playing a scary sound file, or having the Mesh of a bat fly around the room, or playing a video, etc. The end result would be that any time the player enters that doorway, something specific happens.

To give you another example, let's say you have a racing game. You could place a Trigger Volume at the finish line so that when the player reaches that point it will trigger the Event that handles the end of the race.

Pain Causing Volumes

A *Pain Causing Volume* will cause Damage to an Actor who enters that volume. For example, you could surround a fire with a Pain Causing Volume so that a player takes Damage if they "enter the fire." Damage is a built-in concept in the Unreal Engine, and you can use Blueprints to define what happens when an Actor takes Damage, such as subtracting from their health based on the amount of Damage done.

The first property of Pain Causing Volumes is simply called *Pain Causing.* This will determine if the Volume will actually apply Damage to Actors that enter it. By unchecking this, it will disable the Pain Causing feature of the Volume.

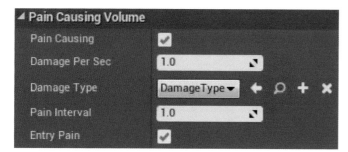

Figure 4.8.3 – Properties of a Pain Causing Volume

The next property is *Damage Per Second*. This determines the rate at which the Actor inside the Volume is damaged. But note that it does not determine the *interval* at which the Damage is applied. That is set by the *Pain Interval* property.

For example, with them both set to 1, every second a point of Damage will be applied. If the Pain Interval was changed to 0.5, then Damage would be applied every half-second. However, now only half a point of Damage would be applied each time, so that, overall, the Actor is still only receiving 1 point of Damage per second. If the Pain Interval was changed to 2, then Damage would only be applied every 2 seconds, but it would apply 2 points of Damage each time.

An easy way to calculate how much Damage will be applied at each interval is to multiply the two values together. So if the Damager Per Second is 2, and the Pain Interval is 4, then 8 points of Damage will be applied at each interval.

The *Damage Type* allows you to change the overall way that Damage by the Volume is handled by the Engine. However, in almost all cases, you will just want to leave this on the default.

The *Entry Pain* property specifies whether or not Damage should be applied to the Actor immediately upon entering the Volume. With Entry Pain checked, the Actor will receive Damage immediately and then again after every interval. With Entry Pain unchecked, the Actor will not receive any Damage until the first interval has elapsed.

Kill ZVolume

The *Kill ZVolume* will destroy any Actor that enters it. It is useful for defining any places in your Level that mean instant death. For example, if you had a pit of lava in your Level, you might want to surround the pit with a Kill ZVolume. Or if you wanted to kill a player that had fallen off a ledge into a bottomless pit, you could use a Kill ZVolume.

You can define in Blueprints what should happen when the player is destroyed, such as displaying a Game Over menu.

Physics Volume

The *Physics Volume* allows you to change the physics of the space within the Volume.

Its first property is *Terminal Velocity*. Terminal velocity is the maximum speed that something can reach when it's falling, or, put another way, the maximum speed something can reach due to the forces of gravity.

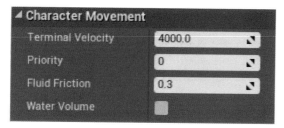

Figure 4.8.4 – Properties of a Physics Volume

When something falls, if nothing interrupts the fall, the object will continue to accelerate until it reaches the Terminal Velocity, and then it will no longer accelerate; it will fall at a constant rate of speed. In the real world, all objects falling toward the Earth have the same terminal velocity. But this value will be different on other planets that have different amounts of gravity.

So you could use the Terminal Velocity property to better mimic an alien world, or you could use it to produce other effects. For example, reducing the Terminal Velocity of the Volume to something really low, so that objects fall very slowly through it.

The next property is *Priority*. This is used when two Physics Volumes are overlapping, in order to determine which Volumes' settings should be used for that overlapping space. The higher the value, the higher the priority. So if a Physics Volume with a Priority of 0 overlapped a Physics Volume with a Priority of 1, only the settings for the Volume with a Priority of 1 would be honored within the overlapping space.

The next property is *Fluid Friction*. This is used to mimic the friction that occurs when something passes through something semi-solid. For example, trying to walk through water is a lot more difficult than walking through air, because there is a lot more friction. Walking through mud is more difficult than walking through water. The higher the Fluid Friction, the slower that objects will pass through it.

Last, is the *Water Volume* property. This specifies whether or not the space that the Volume is defining is supposed to be occupied by water or a water-based liquid. For example, this could be used in Blueprints to specify that anytime the character is within a "water" volume that the character should begin to swim.

4.9 Chapter 4 Quiz

1. If you drag a new mesh Actor into your Level and position it in the air, what two default settings of a mesh must be changed so that the mesh will fall to the ground when the Level begins?

2. True or False: Making copies of a Brush Actor will increase the memory requirements for that Level.

3. How do you select just a single surface of a Brush?

4. In Unreal, when a mesh has different Materials applied to different sections of its surface, what are those different sections called?

5. True or False: When you scale an Actor, any Material applied to it automatically gets scaled as well.

6. In Unreal, what is the best type of Light Actor to use to represent sunlight?

7. In Unreal, what is the best type of Light Actor to use to represent the light from a light bulb?

8. In Unreal, what is the best type of Light Actor to use to represent the light from a flashlight?

9. In Unreal, what is the best type of Light Actor to use to represent the light that is reflected off the atmosphere?

10. What Actor is used to add a blue sky and a sun disc to your Level?

11. True or False: All Components can also function as Actors on their own.

12. In Unreal, what do you call a 3D area of space that is invisible to the player and serves a specific purpose depending on its type?

13. If you wanted to have a small fire in your Level apply Damage to an Actor, what is the easiest way to accomplish this?

Answers

1. The Actor's Mobility will need to be changed from Static to Moveable. Also, the Simulate Physics property will need to be set to True.

2. True

3. First, make sure the Brush isn't currently selected. Then click on the individual surface you wish to select.

4. Elements

5. True

6. Directional Light

7. Point Light

8. Spot Light

9. Sky Light

10. Atmospheric Fog

11. False. While many Components are also Actors themselves, some, such as the Rotating Movement Component, are not.

12. Volume

13. Surround the fire with a Pain Causing Volume.

5

Blueprints ⌄

5.1 Introduction to Blueprints

In the Unreal Engine, a *Blueprint* is an Asset that contains data and instructions.

So far, this book has mainly shown you how to construct environments that can be used for games. But the environment is only one half of a game. The other half is the logic that determines how the environment can be interacted with and how the game is actually played. This is where Blueprints come into play.

Using Blueprints, you can keep track of health, energy, score, etc. You can also specify game logic, like the requirements for completing a puzzle, what happens when that puzzle is complete, what happens when you shoot an enemy, and so on.

Level Blueprint vs Blueprint Classes

There are two main types of Blueprints - The Level Blueprint and Blueprint Classes.

A *Level Blueprint* is used to hold data and instructions for a particular Level. It might hold data such as the time remaining to complete the Level, or the number of keys you've collected in that Level, and so on. It's also used to store instructions that pertain only to that Level. For example, let's say there was a spot in a Level where there was a bridge and when the player crosses that bridge, a meteor flies across the sky. If that's a one-time unique occurrence just for that spot in that Level, it would make sense to store those instructions in the Level Blueprint for that Level.

Blueprint Classes are a way to turn any Actor or Asset into a Blueprint. This allows you to create objects with custom traits and behaviors. Let's say, again, that you are building a haunted house. And let's say you want to have a chair that floats up and down. Let's also say that you want your character to be able to shoot the chair and, eventually, destroy it. You can achieve all of this by creating a Blueprint Class out of the chair Mesh.

Within the Blueprint, you could specify that the chair should move straight up and down, over and over again, starting from wherever it is placed in the Level. You could also specify that it should contain a variable called Health with a default value of 100. You could also say that any time the chair was hit by a projectile, that 10 should be subtracted from its Health. Finally, you could specify that if the Health of the chair ever gets to 0 or below, that the chair should be destroyed.

One of the great things about Blueprint Classes is that you can use them to create as many copies, or instances, of your creation as you want. Using the haunted chair as an example - once you completed the Blueprint, it would be available to you in the Content Browser, and then each time you dragged it into the Viewport, it would create a new instance of the chair. Each chair would float up and down, starting from the position they were placed, and each chair would have their own copy of the Health variable. So if you damaged one of the chairs, its Health would be 90, while the other chairs would still have a Health of 100.

Level Blueprint Editor

To open a Level Blueprint, go up to the Toolbar and expand the menu of the Blueprints button. Then click on "Open Level Blueprint." This will open the *Level Blueprint Editor*.

Event Graph

Inside the Level Blueprint Editor is the *Event Graph*. The Event Graph is the area of a Blueprint where you script the logic. If you're a programmer, the logic can be scripted in pure code using C++. However, Epic Games has developed a visual scripting system that allows non-programmers to script logic and can be convenient even for experienced programmers.

Nodes

The scripting system works by using various *Nodes*, that each serve a specific purpose, and connecting those Nodes together. By default, the Level Blueprint starts off with two commonly used Nodes in the Graph. They are disabled to start with, but can be used right away by connecting them to another Node.

The first Node is the *Event BeginPlay Node*. An *Event Node* is a Node that is activated when a certain event occurs. So an Event BeginPlay Node, inside of a Level Blueprint, will be activated by the event of the Level first starting. You can recognize an Event Node by its top strip which will be the color red and will have an icon of an arrow inside of a diamond symbol.

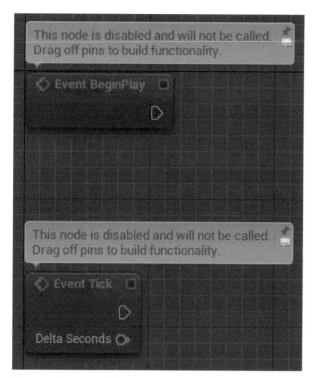

Figure 5.1.1 – The Event BeginPlay Node and Event Tick Node start in the Level Blueprint by default

The second default Node is also an Event Node. The *Event Tick Node* is a Node that is activated on every tick of gameplay. Before every frame of the game is drawn on the screen, any logic connected to the Event Tick Node will be executed. This is useful in situations where you need to constantly check certain conditions that, when met, will have an immediate effect on the game, such as the main character colliding with something harmful.

Pins and Wires

The icons along the left and/or right sides of Nodes are called *pins*. Pins on the left side of a Node are *input pins* and pins on the right side of a Node are *output pins*. Pins are used to input/output data to and from Nodes and to specify the order in which Nodes should be executed.

Pins can be connected to one another with *wires*. To create a wire, left-click on a pin and then drag the mouse while still holding the LMB. This will drag a wire out of that pin. If you hover over another pin and release the LMB, it will connect the end of the wire to that pin.

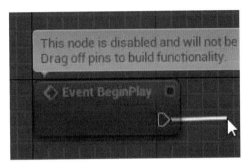

Figure 5.1.2 – Wires can be dragged out of pins

Pins with a white icon that looks like a Play button are *execution pins*. Execution pins on the left side of a Node are *input execution pins*. When a wire connected to an input execution pin is activated, it will trigger execution of that Node. Execution pins on the right side of a Node are *output execution pins*. Wires connected to an output execution pin will activate once that Node has finished executing. Output execution pins can only be connected to input execution pins and vice-versa. By chaining Nodes together through their execution pins, you can define a series of Nodes that should be executed, one after the other, every time the first Node in the series is activated. The first Node in a chain will always be an Event Node.

Pins with a circular icon are *data pins*. Data pins are used to pass data between Nodes. Output data pins can only be connected to input data pins and vice-versa. Whatever data is contained in the output data pin gets sent to the input data pin it is connected to.

Adding Nodes

To add a new Node to the Event Graph, you will need to select that Node from the Node Menu. The Node Menu can be brought up by right-clicking on any empty space in the Graph, or by releasing the LMB over any empty space when dragging out a wire from an output execution pin. When doing the latter, the Node you add will automatically be connected to the wire.

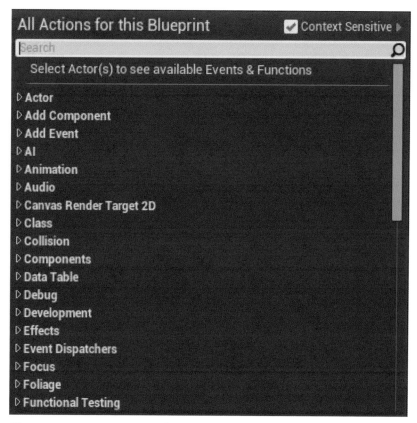

Figure 5.1.3 – You can add Nodes from the Node Menu

There are many Nodes available to choose from in the Node Menu. They are organized into categories, but if you know at least part of the name of the Node you're looking for, you can use the search box at the top of the Node Menu to search for it.

Compiling

Before you can test any new logic you have created, you must compile the Blueprint. *Compiling* just means that the Engine will convert the logic into machine code that the computer can understand. In order to compile the Blueprint, simply go up to the toolbar of the Blueprint Editor and click the Compile button. If there is any new logic that hasn't been compiled yet, the Compile button will contain a question-mark icon.

Figure 5.1.4 – The Compile button

Simple Blueprint Example

Here is a simple, albeit non-practical, example of a Blueprint to help you gain familiarity. The following is a Level Blueprint whose logic specifies that the game should exit two seconds after the Level begins:

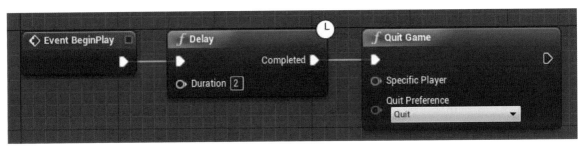

Figure 5.1.5 – This logic will cause the game to exit two seconds after the Level begins

As mentioned earlier, the Event BeginPlay Node will be executed when the Level first begins. As a consequence, any Nodes connected to the Event BeginPlay Node through execution pins will get executed as well.

The Event BeginPlay Node is connected to a *Delay Node*. The Delay Node is a *Function Node*. Function Nodes are light blue and have an icon of a lowercase "f." A Function Node is a Node that performs a specific task when executed. The task of a Delay Node is to wait for a specified amount of seconds before passing execution on to the next Node. In this example, a value of 2 seconds has been specified. A Delay Node doesn't delay the execution of all logic in the game, just within the flow of wires it's connected to.

After a two-second delay, execution will pass to the *Quit Game Node* which will cause the game to exit.

5.2 Variables

Variables are what Blueprints use to store data. Just like in algebra, where you might use a variable named X to store a number, you can use variables in Unreal to store data. But in Unreal, variables can hold other kinds of data in addition to numbers, such as text.

To create a variable in Unreal, first look on the left side of the Blueprint Editor for the *My Blueprint* tab. Within the My Blueprint tab is a Variables sub-tab. Clicking on the plus sign on that tab will create a new variable which can then be named.

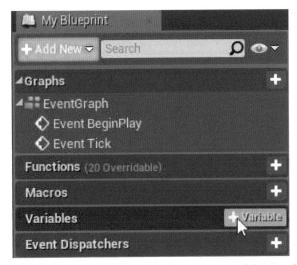

Figure 5.2.1 – You can add new variables in the My Blueprint tab

Data Types

A variable's *data type* determines what kind of data it can hold. One way of setting the data type is to click on the rectangle to the left of the variable's name, and then choose the data type from the menu that appears. The menu will contain a list of all the basic data types in Unreal. Each data type can be identified by a unique color.

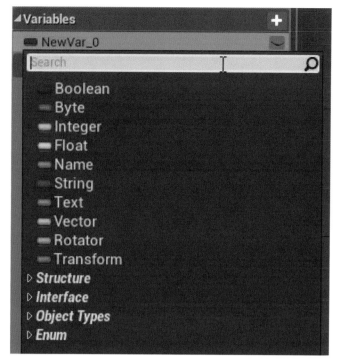

Figure 5.2.2 – Each data type in Unreal can be identified by a unique color

The first one on the list is the *Boolean* data type, which is identified by the color red in Unreal. A Boolean data type is simply used to hold a value of *True* or *False* and those are the only two values it can hold. Because of this, a Boolean data type takes up very little space in memory.

The next three data types in the list - Byte, Integer, and Float - are all used to hold numbers. But they each hold different kinds of numbers and each take up different amounts of space in memory as a result.

A *Byte* is the smallest data type of the three, meaning it takes up the least amount of space in memory. This is because a Byte can only store a whole number between 0 and 255, inclusive. So if you needed a variable to store, for example, some choice that the player makes in the game, and there are only a limited amount of choices the player can make, a Byte might be a good data type to use to store this choice, with each number corresponding to one of the choices the player could make.

Like the Byte, the *Integer* is used to store whole numbers. But unlike the Byte, it doesn't have the restriction of that value being only between 0-255. Because of this, however, it will also use more memory than a Byte.

Float is short for "floating point number." A "floating point" is just another name for a decimal point. So a Float is used to hold numbers that have a decimal place. Unlike the Integer, it can be used to store numbers that aren't whole, such as 3.5, or 24.743, etc. Because of this, it requires more memory than the Integer data type.

The next three data types are used to store text. The largest of the three is the *Text* data type. Because this requires the most amount of memory of the three, it should only be used for its specific purpose, which is to store data that will be displayed on the screen to the player. The Text data type is useful for displaying text because it has, among other things, localization features, which allows it to display text in a way that is custom for that player's region or language.

The *String* data type is used to store text that you can perform manipulation functions on. These functions include extracting a substring of text from the larger portion, changing the case of the text, meaning uppercase or lowercase, reversing the text, and so on. The String type is smaller than the Text type, so if you might have a need to perform these functions on the text, and the text isn't going to be displayed on the screen, you would store the text in a String variable.

The smallest of these three data types is the *Name* data type. The Name type doesn't have the localization or other features that the Text data type has to display text on the screen, and it also doesn't have the manipulation functions of the String data type. However, it does take up the least amount of memory of the three. So you would use the Name data type for any text that doesn't require the features of the String or Text data types.

The *Vector* data type is used to store three Float values. This is useful for defining a point in space, an RGB value, or anything that is defined with three values.

The *Rotator* data type is used to store numbers that describe an object's rotation in 3D space.

The *Transform* data type is used to hold data that describes an object's position, rotation, and scale in 3D space.

Get Node

A *Get Node* is a Node whose only purpose is to output the value of a variable. It will contain just a single pin, an output data pin. It has no execution pins. A Get Node can be thought of as always active, because it will output the current value of the variable, every tick of gameplay, to whatever pin it is connected to.

To create a Get Node for a specific variable, left-click on the variable in the My Blueprint tab and drag it into the Event Graph. When you release the LMB, click on "Get" from the menu that appears. This will create a Get Node. Another way to do this is to hold down the *Ctrl* key when dragging the variable into the Graph, and then when you let go of the mouse, it will automatically create a Get Node for the variable.

Figure 5.2.3 – A Get Node for a Float variable named "Delay Duration"

Set Node

A *Set Node* is used to change the value of a variable. It contains an input data pin which is used to specify what value the variable should be changed to. The value will be changed once the Node is activated through its input execution pin. The Node also contains an output data pin so the new value can be passed on to another Node if you wish.

To create a Set Node for a specific variable, left-click on the variable in the My Blueprint tab and drag it into the Event Graph. When you release the LMB, click on "Set" from the menu that appears. This will create a Set Node. Another way to do this is to hold down the *Alt* key when dragging the variable into the Graph, and then when you let go of the mouse, it will automatically create a Set Node for the variable.

Figure 5.2.4 – A Set Node for a Float variable named "Delay Duration"

Default Value

A *default value* is a value that will be assigned to a variable as soon as the variable is created. The default value can be set in the Details Panel, on the right side of the Blueprint Editor, under the "Default Value" category. If you see the text "Please compile the blueprint" it means that you haven't compiled the Blueprint since that variable was created. Once you compile the Blueprint, that text will go away and a box will appear where you can enter the default value.

Figure 5.2.5 – When you create a new variable, you will need to compile the Blueprint before you can give that variable a default value

Updated Blueprint Example

Expanding on the Blueprint example from the previous section, here is an example of using a variable to specify the duration that the Delay Node should delay:

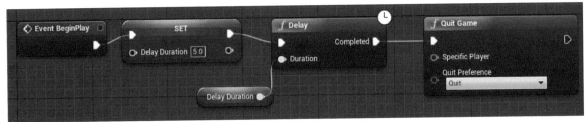

Figure 5.2.6 – The Duration property of the Delay Node is now set by a variable

The Set Node sets a Float variable named "Delay Duration" to a value of 5.0. A Get Node for the "Delay Duration" variable passes the value of that variable to the Delay Node. So now, the Delay Node will delay for 5 seconds instead of the 2 seconds that were "hardcoded" into the Node in the previous example.

Variable Properties

In addition to the default value, there are other properties of variables that you can set in the Details Panel. Some data types will have different properties than others.

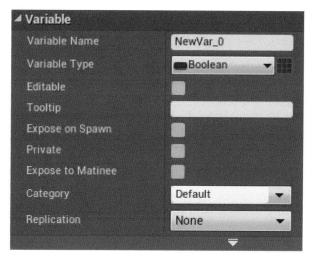

Figure 5.2.7 – Properties of a Boolean variable

The first two properties, *Variable Name* and *Variable Type*, are the same properties that you can edit in the My Blueprint tab, so the Details Panel is just another place where you can set them.

The *Editable* property will be covered in the section on Blueprint Classes.

The *Tooltip* property allows you to give a detailed explanation of what the variable is and what it is used for. This is useful not only when you are working on teams - so that the people you are working with can more quickly understand what you've created - but also for yourself, so that when you come back to the variable at a later time, you can quickly remember its use.

To create a tooltip, just type the message into the Tooltip box, and when the variable is hovered over in the My Blueprint tab, or when a Set node for that variable is hovered over, it will display the tooltip message that you've created.

The *Expose on Spawn* and *Expose to Matinee* properties involve more advanced topics and won't be covered in this book.

The *Private* property determines if other Blueprints can access the variable. With this unchecked, other Blueprints will be able to access the variable. With it checked and set to Private, other Blueprints would not be able to access the variable.

The *Category* property allows you to group your variables into categories if you wish. This is for organizational purposes within the Editor. To place a variable into a category, select an existing one from the dropdown or create a new one by typing its name into the box. Once a variable has been placed into a category, it will appear under a heading for that category in the My Blueprint tab.

The next two properties are *Slider Range* and *Value Range*. These properties are only for numerical data types.

Starting with the Value Range property, this allows you to set a minimum and maximum value that the variable is allowed to contain. If you set the Value Range to 0 to 10, you won't be able to set the variable to anything other than those numbers and the numbers in-between. If you go down to the Default Value, for example, and try to set that to 11, it won't let you.

The Slider Range property determines what value you can set the variable to when using a slider. If you set the range to 3 to 5, for example, and try to use the slider on the Default Value to set the number, it will only go between 3 and 5. But if you enter a number manually, you can still enter any number not restricted by the Value Range or the limits of the data type itself.

The *Replication* property is used in multiplayer games that are running over a network. This specifies whether or not the variable should be replicated over the network. So if it's a variable that would affect all the players in the game, it would need to be replicated over the network. But if it's a variable that only affects an individual player, it would probably not need to be replicated over the network.

5.3 Arrays

An *array* is a list of variables of the same data type. You can have an array of Integers, an array of Strings, and so on.

This is useful whenever you need to store a group of something. For example, you could use an array of Integers to store the combination to a safe. Or you could use an array of Strings to store the dialogue of a character for a certain scene.

To create an array, first create a regular variable with the data type you want the array to use, and then click on the grid icon to the right of the Variable Type property in the Details Panel.

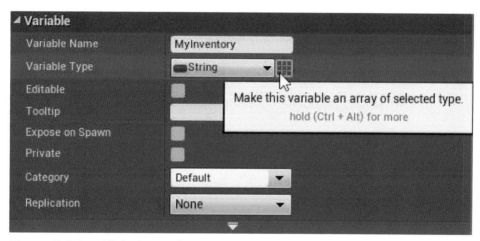

Figure 5.3.1 – Click the grid icon to make a variable an array

Arrays are made up of slots that each store one of the values of the list. The proper term for one of these slots is an *index*. Arrays in Unreal are "zero-based" which means the first index is 0. So the second index is 1, the third index is 2, and so on. Each value stored in the array is known as an *element* of the array.

ForEachLoop Node

The *ForEachLoop Node* is used to iterate through the elements of an array. It has an input pin called *Array* where you can input the array you wish to use. It has an output execution pin called *Loop Body* that will be activated once for each element in the array. Each time the Loop Body pin fires, the Node's *Array Element* pin will contain the value of the current element, and the Array Index pin will contain the index number of the current element. The output execution pin *Completed* will fire once all the elements have been iterated through.

The following example will loop through an array of Strings named "My Inventory" and output each value to the screen:

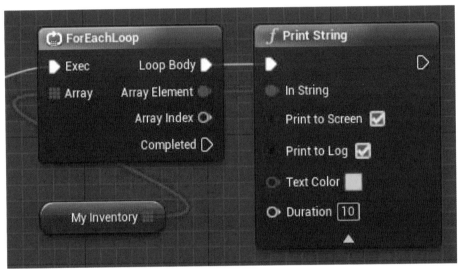

Figure 5.3.2 – The ForEachLoop Node will loop through every element of an array

Add Node

The *Add Node* can be used to add another element to the end of an array. It has an input pin for the array itself and an input pin for the variable containing the value to add.

In the following example, whatever value the variable "New Item" contains will be added to the end of an array named "My Inventory" whenever the *P* key is pressed on the keyboard:

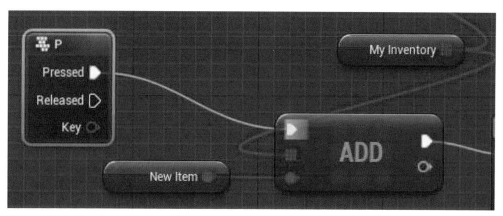

Figure 5.3.3 – Pressing P will cause New Item to be added to the end of the My Inventory array

Insert Node

The Add Node will add a new element to the end of the array, but to add a new element somewhere in the middle you need to use the *Insert Node*. It has a pin to specify the array, a pin to specify the value you want to add, and a pin to specify at which index the value should be inserted.

Figure 5.3.4 – The Insert Node

When a value is inserted, the length of the array increases by one, all the values at the specified index and above get moved one index higher, and then the new value is assigned to the specified index. So the Insert Node inserts values in-between other values without erasing any data.

Set Array Element Node

If you want to replace the value of a certain index, you need to use the *Set Array Element Node*. Unlike the Insert Node, this Node will overwrite the value at the specified index and won't change the location of any of the other values.

Figure 5.3.5 – The Set Array Element Node

The Set Array Element Node has a *Size to Fit* pin. As an example, let's say that at the time the Node fires, the array being used has 4 elements (indices 0 to 3). Also, let's say you specify that you want the new value to go into index 6. If Size to Fit is False, this won't work, because index 6 doesn't exist. The game won't crash, the array simply won't change in any way. But if Size to Fit were True in this scenario, the length of the array would increase to 7, so that there is an index 6. Index 6 would get set to the new value specified, and indices 4 and 5 would simply remain empty.

Removing Elements From an Array

When you want to remove elements from an array, there are a few ways to do this. The *Clear Node* simply deletes all the elements of an array. The *Remove Index Node* will delete the element at the specified index, and then shift any values at higher indexes down one. The *Remove Item Node* deletes elements based on their values, deleting any element whose value matches the one specified. The Remove Item Node also has a Boolean pin that outputs True or False based on if any matches were found.

Figure 5.3.6 – The Clear Node

Figure 5.3.7 – The Remove Index Node

Figure 5.3.8 – The Remove Item Node

Contains Item Node

When you just want to know whether or not an array contains a certain value, you can use the *Contains Item Node*. You specify the value you want to search for and it will output True if that value was found and False if it was not.

Figure 5.3.9 – The Contains Item Node

Find Item Node

If you need to know the index that a certain value is located at, you can use the *Find Item Node*. This will return the index of the first element of the array that matches the value specified. If no match is found, this will return a value of -1.

Figure 5.3.10 – The Find Item Node

Length Node & Last Index Node

You can use the *Length Node* when you want to know how many elements an array has, and the *Last Index Node* when you want to know its highest index number. Because arrays in Unreal Engine are zero-based, the last index of an array will always be one less than its length.

Figure 5.3.11 – The Length Node

Figure 5.3.12 – The Last Index Node

5.4 Functions

A *function* is a procedure or routine meant to carry out a specific task or series of tasks. Functions are not unique to Unreal Engine. A function is a concept that comes from mathematics and computer science. In computer science and programming, a function is a specific block of code. By extension, in Unreal Engine, a function is a specific Event Graph of Nodes. The entire Event Graph for a function gets *encapsulated* (contained) within a single Node that can then be used without having to worry about the details inside it.

To create a new function, go to the My Blueprint tab, look for the Functions category, and then click on the Add button. Whenever you create a new function, it will automatically open that function's Event Graph and add its *Entry Node*. The Entry Node is the Node that will fire whenever the function is called.

Figure 5.4.1 – New functions can be added in the My Blueprint tab

Figure 5.4.2 – The Entry Node for a function named "Welcome Message"

Function I/O

Functions can have inputs and outputs so that data can be passed into and out of the function. To add an input or output, go to the Details Panel and click on the New button under the Inputs or Outputs category, depending on which you want to create. You can then define the name and data type of the input/output.

Figure 5.4.3 – Clicking on these New buttons will create either an input or output for your function

When an input is created, looking "outside" of the function, at its single-node encapsulated form, you will see the input created as an input pin. "Inside" of the function, the data that gets passed to that input pin can be retrieved through a corresponding output pin that gets added to the Entry Node.

Creating an output variable will create a *Return Node* within the function. The Return Node will always be the last Node of a function, and it will contain input pins for each of your output variables so that you can pass that data back out of the function (these will appear as output pins on the Function Node itself).

Function Example

As an example, here's a function that takes a name as input and then outputs a message using that name:

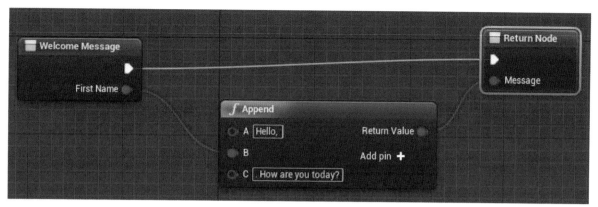

Figure 5.4.4 – The "inside" of the Welcome Message function

It has one input - a String variable named "First Name" - and one output - a String variable named "Message." It retrieves First Name from the Entry Node and passes that to an Append Node where it combines the name with other Strings to form a greeting. That greeting is then passed to the Return Node. Here is an example of the function in use:

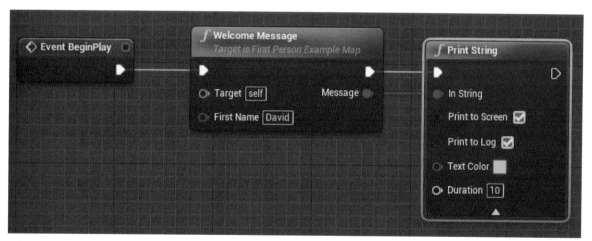

Figure 5.4.5 – The Welcome Message function in use

As soon as the Level begins it will call the Welcome Message function. The name "David" is passed in as the value of First Name. This is the value that will be retrieved from the Entry Node within the function. The message that is created inside the function, and gets passed to the Return Node, is the message that is being retrieved here and then passed to the Print String Node.

Advantages of Using Functions

Using functions has many advantages. The main advantage is *reusability*. For example, if you wanted to use the above Welcome Message function dozens of times throughout your game, with several different characters with different names, you don't want to have to write the logic every single time, for each character, every time it is used. It would be easier to just write it once and be able to use it over and over again.

Another advantage of functions is *editability*, meaning it is much easier to make changes. For example, let's say you later decide you want the wording of the welcome message to be slightly different. If you had the logic in dozens of places, without using a function, you would have to manually try and find each of those places and then edit each one individually. But with a function, you only need to make the change in one place - in the function itself.

A third advantage is *reliability*. If you use a function that's already been used, and thus tested, over and over again, there's a much better chance that that function is free of mistakes than logic you just wrote. For example, many of the built-in functions in Unreal Engine have now been used repeatedly by numerous companies and developers and thus any bugs they may have once contained have already been reported and fixed.

A fourth advantage of functions is *readability*. While the Welcome Message function example is very small, functions could contain hundreds or even thousands of Nodes. But no matter how many nodes a function contains, it will always get condensed down into just one Node. So by hiding away the "guts" of your logic in this way, it makes it much easier to understand the logic of your game at a high level.

Function Properties

The *Description* property is used to briefly explain what the function does. Whatever this is set to will appear in the tool tip message that pops-up whenever you hover over a function. So if you come back to this function later, or someone you're working with comes across it, this makes it much easier to quickly understand what a function does without having to open it up and analyze its logic.

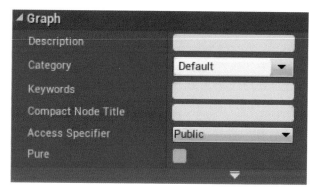

Figure 5.4.6 – Function properties

The *Category* property is used to organize your custom-made functions. For example, you could assign a function to a category called "String" and then in the My Blueprint tab, it will group the function under that category, along with any other functions you assign to that category.

The *Keywords* property can be used to add a list of keywords to the function which can be useful if you search for the function later.

If you give the *Compact Node Title* property a value, it will display the Function Node in a compact form, with the value you entered being displayed in the background.

The *Access Specifier* property is used to specify what Blueprints are allowed to call this function. With this set to *Public*, any Blueprint is allowed to call this function. With this set to *Private*, only the Blueprint that the function belongs to is allowed to call it. For example, if a function was created in the Level Blueprint, and Access Specifier is set to Private, you will only be able to call the function from the Level Blueprint and no other.

The *Protected* setting is like the Private setting, except that the function can also be called from Blueprints derived from the owning Blueprint. Derived Blueprints will be discussed in the chapter on Players & Input.

The final property deals with the concept of *Pure* vs. *Impure* functions. A Pure function cannot modify any of the variables of its Blueprint, while an Impure function can.

5.5 Flow Control

In the Node Menu, under "Utilities," there is a category called *Flow Control*. This category contains several different Nodes that you can use to control the flow of execution in your Blueprints. This is essential to creating logic.

Branch Node

The first node in the list is the *Branch Node*. The Branch Node takes in a Boolean value as its input and then continues execution either through the True output execution pin if the Boolean value is True, or through the False output execution pin if the Boolean value is False.

Figure 5.5.1 – The Branch Node

For example, when the player tries to open a door, you could have a Branch Node with a Boolean variable that stores whether or not the player has the key. You could connect the False pin to a Node that will play the sound of a locked door trying to be opened and connect the True pin to the sound of a door being unlocked.

Do N Node

The *Do N Node* means "Do N times" where "N" is the number of times this Node should allow execution to pass through it before it begins to block execution. For example, if N is 5, then the first 5 times execution flows into the Enter pin it will flow out of the Exit pin. However, the 6th time and beyond that, the flow will not continue out of the Exit pin.

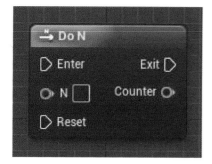

Figure 5.5.2 – The Do N Node

So execution will be blocked in a Do N Node after the Nth time the Node has been activated, unless execution flows into the Reset pin of the Node. When execution flows into the Reset pin, the counter will be reset to 0 and the Node will be able to execute N more times.

The Counter pin will output an Integer representing the number of times the Do N node has been activated since the game began or since the last time the Node was reset.

DoOnce Node

The *DoOnce Node* is just like a Do N Node where N = 1. With the exception that with the DoOnce Node, you have the option to have the Node start closed. By having the Node start closed, this means that execution must flow through the Reset pin before execution will flow through the Completed pin, even the first time.

Figure 5.5.3 – The DoOnce Node

DoOnce MultiInput Node

The *DoOnce MultiInput Node* is like the DoOnce Node except that it allows for multiple In/Out pairs. Additional pairs can be added using the "Add pin" button at the bottom. So if execution flows into the A In pin, it will flow out of the A Out pin. If execution flows into the A In pin a second time, without a reset, nothing will happen, but execution will still be able to flow through the B pins and the C pins.

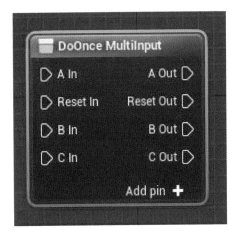

Figure 5.5.4 – The DoOnce MultiInput Node

If execution flows into the Reset In pin, all of the pairs will get Reset. The DoOnce MultiInput Node also differs from the DoOnce Node in that it has a Reset Out pin that will be executed when the Reset In pin is executed.

FlipFlop Node

The *FlipFlop Node* simply alternates between having execution flow out of the A pin or the B pin every time the Node is activated. The first time execution flows into the FlipFlop Node, it will flow out of the A pin, and the second time execution flows into the FlipFlop Node, it will flow out of the B pin, and then the third time, it will flow out of the A pin again, and so on.

Figure 5.5.5 – The FlipFlop Node

The FlipFlop Node has a Boolean output called *Is A* that will output a value of True if execution is currently being routed through the A pin, and False if execution is being routed through the B pin.

ForLoop Node

With a *ForLoop Node*, the Loop Body execution output pin is fired a certain number of times, starting from an Integer defined by the First Index, and then increasing by 1 until it gets to the Integer defined by the Last Index. The Index pin will output an Integer specifying the index of the current loop. The Completed pin will be executed after the final loop is completed.

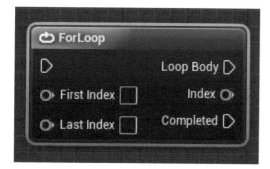

Figure 5.5.6 – The ForLoop Node

ForLoopWithBreak Node

The *ForLoopWithBreak Node* is just like the ForLoop Node, except that it is possible to break the loop before it is finished. If execution flows into the Break pin, the loop will stop immediately and the remaining loops will not be executed.

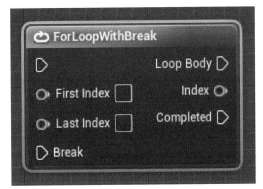

Figure 5.5.7 – The ForLoopWithBreak Node

Gate Node

A *Gate Node* is a Node that can be set to opened or closed. When the Gate is open, execution flow entering the Enter pin will flow out of the Exit pin. When the Gate is closed, any execution flow entering the Node will stop there, and the Exit pin will not fire.

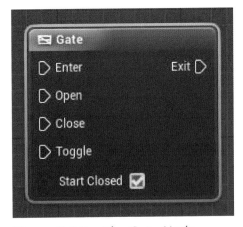

Figure 5.5.8 – The Gate Node

The next three input pins are used to set the status of the Gate. Any time execution flows into the Open pin, it will open the Gate, and any time execution flows into the Close pin, it will close the Gate. If execution flows into the Toggle pin it will set the status to whatever it is currently not. So if the Gate was open, the Toggle pin would close it, and if the Gate was closed, the Toggle pin would open it. The Start Closed property will determine whether the Gate starts out Open or Closed.

MultiGate Node

With a *MultiGate Node*, execution enters a single execution input pin, but it will flow out of only one of the execution output pins. You can use the Add pin button to add as many execution output pins as you like.

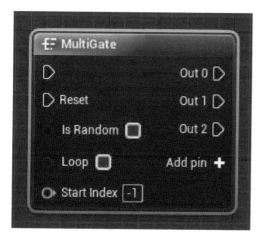

Figure 5.5.9 – The MultiGate Node

If Is Random is unchecked or set to False, then execution will flow out of the output pins in sequential order, starting at the Start Index. With a Start Index of -1, it's the same as saying that you're not specifying a Start Index, so it will just go with the default which is 0. Loop will determine whether or not the sequence should start over or if the Node should just block further execution flow.

If Is Random is set to True, then instead of going in sequential order, output will flow out of the pins in random order until each pin has been used. At that point, the Node will either need to be reset or start a new loop, depending on what Loop was set to.

Retriggerable Delay Node

The *Retriggerable Delay Node* is just like the Delay Node, except that the delay can be reset or "retriggered" if another pulse enters the execution input pin before the delay has finished counting down. So if the duration of the delay is set to 10 seconds, and the Node is activated, and then after 7 seconds the Node is activated again, the delay will start counting down from 10 again.

Figure 5.5.10 – The Retriggerable Delay Node

Sequence Node

With the *Sequence Node*, every time execution flows into the Node it will flow out of every single one of the output pins. Again, you can use the Add pin button to add as many output pins as you want. When execution flows into the Node, it will fire each of the pins sequentially, however it will do so without any delay, so from the player's perspective it will appear as if each of the pins fired at the same time.

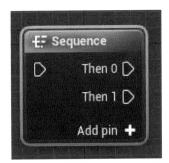

Figure 5.5.11 – The Sequence Node

WhileLoop Node

Once the *WhileLoop Node* has been activated, the Loop Body pin will fire over and over again, as long as the Boolean value connected to the Condition pin is True. Before each loop iteration, it will check the value of Condition, and once the Condition is False it will break the loop and execution will flow out of the Completed pin. It's important to make sure that there is definitely some way for the Condition to eventually evaluate to False, or you will end up with an infinite loop.

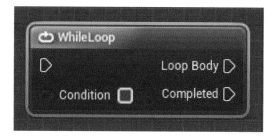

Figure 5.5.12 – The WhileLoop Node

Switches

Switches are a way to route the flow of execution based on the value of whatever variable you pass into the Switch. For example, if you create a *Switch on Int Node*, you can connect an Integer variable to the Selection pin, and then when the Node is activated, it will read in the value of the Integer and based on that value, route execution to one of the output pins.

Figure 5.5.13 – The Switch on Int Node

By default, the only output pin is the Default pin. The Add pin button can be used to create more output pins and will create them starting with the value of the Node's Start Index property, and then incrementing by 1 each time the button is pressed. If you want to delete one of the pins you added, you just need to right-click on that pin and click "Remove execution pin".

You can also do a Switch on other data types as well. For example, you could use the *Switch on Name Node*. This will work the same way as the Switch on Int Node, with the exception that you will need to specify the text to compare against for each of the output pins. You can do that by going over to the Details Panel, expanding the Pin Names property, and entering the text you want each pin to check for.

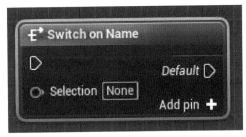

Figure 5.5.14 – The Switch on Name Node

5.6 Accessing Actors Within Blueprints

To really get use out of your Blueprints, you're going to want to be able to access the Actors in your Level in order to be able to read their data, make decisions based on that data, and to manipulate the Actors in different ways.

In order to get access to an Actor within a Blueprint, that Actor needs to be selected in the Level Editor when you right-click in the Event Graph of the Blueprint. When you do so, the Node Menu will have some options at the top relating to that Actor. You can create an Event based on the Actor, you can call a Function on the Actor, and you can also get a reference to the Actor. Note that for this to work, the Context Sensitive checkbox needs to be checked.

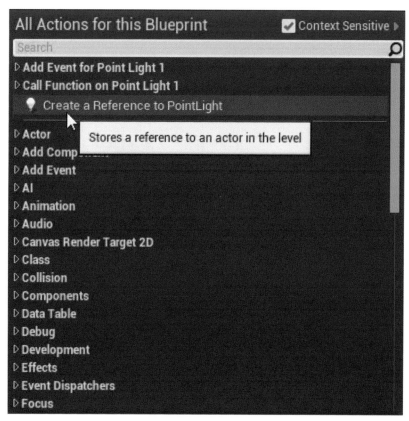

Figure 5.6.1 – You can get a reference to the currently selected Actor through the Node Menu

Getting a Reference to an Actor

The following example uses a reference to a Light Actor to turn that light off two seconds after the Level begins:

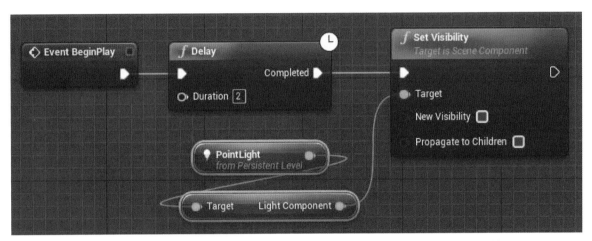

Figure 5.6.2 – This logic will turn a Light Actor off two seconds after the Level begins

The *Set Visibility Node* takes in a Light Component as the "Target" to perform the action on and its New Visibility Boolean will determine whether the Node will set the visibility of the target component to True or False. Note that when connecting the reference to the Light Actor to the Target pin, the Engine automatically created a Node in-between. This is because the Set Visibility function technically sets the visibility of Components, not the Actors themselves, so the Node is just getting the Light Component of the Light Actor so that the Light Component can be passed in as the target component.

Creating an Event From an Actor

To create an Event from an Actor, select the Actor in the Level Editor, open the Node Menu in the Blueprint, make sure Context Sensitive is checked, then select "Add Event for [Actor Name]." From there, if you expand the Collision menu, there will be an option to create an *On Actor Begin Overlap Event*. This Event will fire whenever another Actor overlaps with this Actor. This Event is often used with Trigger Volumes.

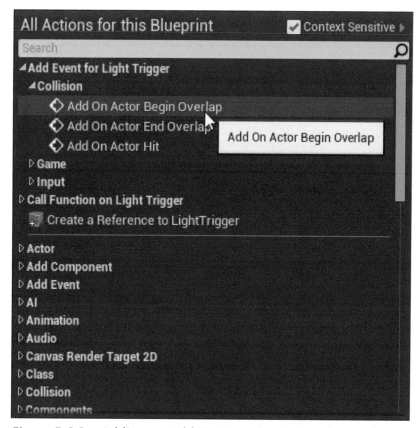

Figure 5.6.3 – Adding an Add On Actor Begin Overlap Node

The following example uses Events to turn a Light on and off when an Actor enters and exits a Trigger Volume named "LightTrigger":

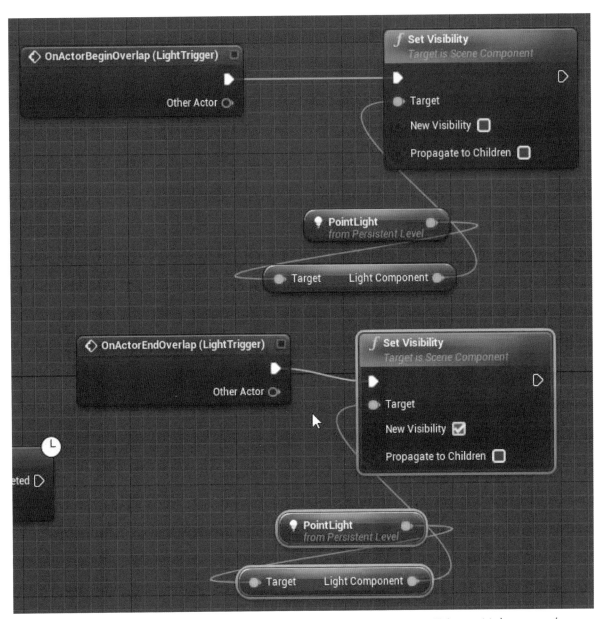

Figure 5.6.4 – This logic will turn a light off when an Actor enters a Trigger Volume and will turn it back on once that Actor leaves the Trigger Volume

5.7 Blueprint Classes

With *Blueprint Classes*, you can create Blueprints out of existing Actors and Assets. By creating a Blueprint from an Actor, you can add data and functionality to that Actor, essentially creating your own custom version of that Actor type.

To create a Blueprint from an Actor, select it, and then in the Details Panel, click on the blue "Blueprint/Add Script" button. Then select the folder path where you want to save the Blueprint, give it a name, and click "Create Blueprint."

⚙ Blueprint/Add Script

Figure 5.7.1 – The Blueprint/Add Script button

So far in this book, the only Blueprints have been Level Blueprints, which only have an Event Graph. But for Blueprints of Actors, there is also a *Viewport* tab and a *Construction Script* tab. The Viewport tab allows you to see what your Actor looks like and also allows you to add Components to it. The Construction Script is something that will be run just before the Actor gets created, so it's useful for performing any initialization you might need to do on the Actor to get it ready for gameplay.

Blueprint Class Example

The following example is a Blueprint that has been created from a Point Light Actor. The logic will cause the Light to turn on and off every second:

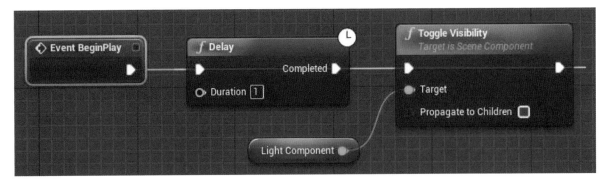

Figure 5.7.2 – This logic will cause a Light Actor to turn on and off every second

The *Toggle Visibility* function is like the Set Visibility function, except instead of using it to specifically set a visibility property to True or False, it will simply toggle the property to the opposite of whatever it's currently set to. So if the visibility was True, the function would set it to False, and vice-versa.

Because this is the Blueprint for the Point Light, the Editor assumed that the Light is the desired target and automatically connected the Light Component of the Light to the Target pin when the Toggle Visibility Node was created.

When the game loads and the Actor is first created in memory, its Event BeginPlay Node will fire. Then the Delay Node will delay flow for one second before the Toggle Visibility Node is activated. The output execution pin of the Toggle Visibility Node has been connected to the input execution pin of the Delay Node. This creates a loop that will cause the Light to turn on and off every second for the duration of the Actor's existence.

Instances

One of the major advantages of Blueprint Classes is that they are reusable. The above Blueprint of a custom Light Actor can be used just like any other Actor. If you browse to it in the Content Browser, you can drag and drop as many instances of it as you want. An *instance* is an individual copy of an object made from a Blueprint.

Editable Variables

When you add a variable to a Blueprint Class, it is, in essence, adding a custom property to that Actor. The following builds upon the earlier example and adds a Float variable named Light Toggle Duration to the Blueprint and uses that variable as the Duration of the Delay Node:

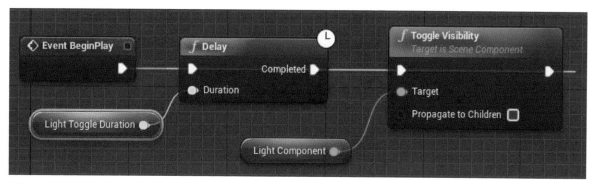

Figure 5.7.3 – A Float variable named Light Toggle Duration has been added to this example

Right now, this isn't doing anything different than it was doing before, but that can be changed by making this variable *Editable*.

There are two ways to make a variable Editable. One way is to use the icon in the My Blueprint tab, which will toggle between the image of an eye open and an image of an eye closed. When the eye is open, that means that the variable is Editable. You can also use the Editable checkbox in the Details Panel to set whether the variable should be Editable or not.

If a variable is set to Editable, its value can be changed in the Level Editor. With the Light Toggle Duration variable set to Editable, if you select an instance of the Light Blueprint in the Level Editor, that variable will now appear in the Details Panel.

Figure 5.7.4 – The variable named Light Toggle Duration now appears in the Details Panel when an instance of the Light Blueprint is selected in the Level

Now you have the ability to easily set a different duration for each instance of the Actor. You could drag in several instances of the Actor, give them each a different Light Toggle Duration, and they will all turn on and off at different rates. This is the power of Blueprint Classes. You can create your own custom Actors and Assets, reuse them as many times as you like, and modify their individual properties.

5.8 Timelines

Timelines are used to create simple animations, such as changing the location, rotation, or color of an object. To add a new Timeline Node, right-click in the graph, select "Add Timeline..." from the bottom of the menu, and give the Timeline a name. To edit a Timeline, double-click it to open it in the *Timeline Editor*.

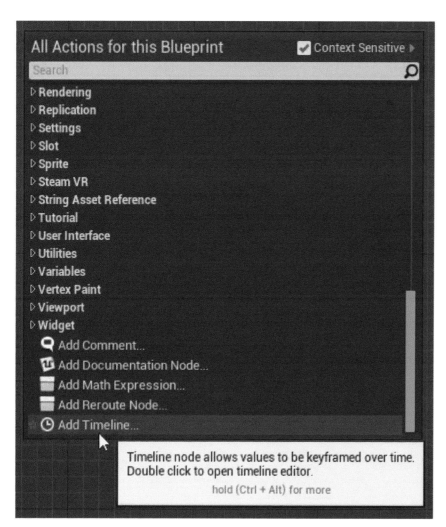

Figure 5.8.1 – A new Timeline Node can be added from the Node Menu

Tracks and Keys

To add a new *track* to a Timeline, use one of the buttons in the upper-left corner of the Timeline Editor. A track is used to specify what value or values the Timeline should be outputting at any given point in time. For example, the first button with the "f" on it is used to add a *Float track* which is used to output single Float values.

Figure 5.8.2 – These buttons are used to add new tracks to a Timeline. The first button creates a Float track.

A track is represented by a graph. The time, in seconds, from the start of the Timeline, is represented horizontally. The value that gets outputted is represented vertically. To specify what value should be outputted at what time, you need to add a *key* to that point on the track's graph. To add a key, hold down *Shift* on the keyboard and left-click in the graph.

To change the placement of a key, either left-click on it and drag it to where you want, or use the boxes at the top of the graph to enter the X and Y values manually. To move around the graph, right-click and drag the mouse. To zoom in-and-out, use the scroll wheel of the mouse, just like in a Blueprint graph.

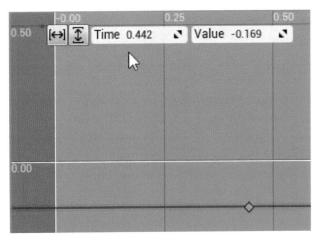

Figure 5.8.3 – The orange diamond in this figure is called a key

Timeline Example

The following is an example of a Timeline that is used to animate a Light Actor, so that its light starts out completely dark, gradually gets brighter, and then gradually gets dimmer again. The Timeline consists of a single Float track that will be used to feed values into the Light's Intensity property:

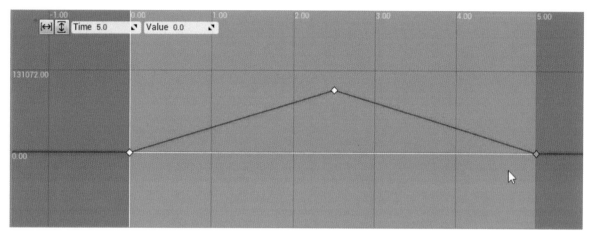

Figure 5.8.4 – The red line in a Timeline is called a curve

The red line is called a *curve*, and represents what value the Timeline Node will output at any given time during the animation. In this case, at the start of the animation, the Timeline Node will output zero, then it will gradually output a higher and higher value, until at 2.5 seconds, it is outputting a value of 100,000. Then, for the next 2.5 seconds, the value gradually decreases, until it reaches zero again.

This value will get outputted from an output pin on the Timeline Node. For each track you create, it will create a new output pin on the Timeline Node that will have the same name as the track and will output the value for that track. In this example, the output of the track is connected to a pin that will set the Intensity property of the Light Component of a Light Actor:

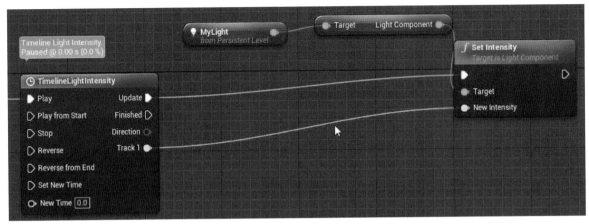

Figure 5.8.5 – Due to the curve of the track created for this Timeline, this logic will cause a light to gradually get brighter, then gradually get dimmer again

When the Play execution pin is activated, it will cause the Timeline to start playing. For the next 5 seconds (the length of the Timeline), for each tick of gameplay, the Update pin will fire, causing the Set Intensity Node to fire. Each time the Set Intensity Node fires, it will receive a different value from the track based on that track's curve and the current playback point of the Timeline.

That's the basics of how Timelines work. You create a curve on a track to output different values across time, and then use those values to update some property during each tick of gameplay.

Other Types of Tracks

The above example used a Float track, but there are other types of tracks as well. If you wanted to create a track to change a Vector value, such as an object's location, you would use the button to the right of the Float track button to create a *Vector track*. By gradually changing an object's location over time, you can create a simple movement animation.

To the right of that, is a button that is used to create an *Event track*, which can be used to specify at what points in time certain Events should fire. To the right of that, is a button used to create a *Color track* which can be used to gradually turn one color into another color.

Add an Existing Curve to a Track

The button to the right of the Color track button can be used to add an already existing curve to a new track. If you select a curve Asset in the Content Browser and then click the button, it will create a new track and add that curve to it.

To add an existing curve to the *current* track, select the curve in the Content Browser, then click the arrow beneath the text "External Curve" to the left of the track you want the curve added to.

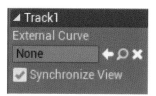

Figure 5.8.6 – Existing curves can be added to a track

To save a curve you create so it can be used again later in the above manner, right-click in the graph and select "Create External Curve" to save the curve as an Asset in the Content Browser.

Timeline Options

To the right of the create track buttons, there are a few options you can set for your Timeline. The first box allows you to set the length of the Timeline. To the right of that is the *Use Last Keyframe?* option. If this is unchecked, the very last tick of the animation will be ignored. This is useful when looping, to prevent skipping in the animation when the loop starts over.

Figure 5.8.7 – Timeline Options

If the *AutoPlay* option is checked, the Timeline will begin playing as soon as the Level (or Actor) is created, even if it's not connected to an Event BeginPlay Node. With the *Loop* option checked, the animation will start over from the beginning once it reaches the end. The *Replicated* option will cause the animation to be replicated across all clients during a multiplayer game.

Timeline Node Pins

When the *Play* pin fires, the Timeline will start playing from its current position. So let's say the Timeline starts at zero, and the Play pin fires, and then two seconds into the animation the *Stop* pin gets executed. At that point, the animation will pause at the two-second mark. If the *Play From Start* pin was executed, the animation would go back to the zero-second mark and play from there. But if the Play pin was executed at that point, the animation would continue playing from the two-second mark.

Figure 5.8.8 – The pins of the Timeline Node

The *Reverse* pin will cause the animation to start playing in Reverse from its current position, and the *Reverse from End* pin will move the animation to the end and then start playing in Reverse from there. The *Set New Time* pin will move the animation to whatever time is specified in the *New Time* pin.

The *Finished* pin fires when the animation is complete. The *Direction* pin will contain a value of either Forward or Reverse, based on which direction the Timeline is playing at that particular moment.

5.9 Chapter 5 Quiz

1. What is the area of a Blueprint where you script the logic called?

2. What Node, inside of a Level Blueprint, will be activated by the Level first starting?

3. What Node is activated before every frame of gameplay?

4. What is it called when the Engine converts the logic of a Blueprint into machine code that the computer can understand?

5. What values can a variable of type Boolean hold?

6. After creating a new variable, what do you need to do before you can set a default value for the variable?

7. What does it mean when a variable's Private property is set to True?

8. What is the index number of the third element of an array?

9. What are four advantages to using functions?

10. What type of Node takes in a Boolean value as its input and then continues execution either through a True output execution pin or a False output execution pin?

11. How do you access an Actor within the Level Blueprint?

12. How do you create a Blueprint out of an existing Actor?

13. What kind of Node can be used to produce simple animations, by outputting a stream of values over time?

Answers

1. Event Graph

2. Event BeginPlay Node

3. Event Tick Node

4. compiling

5. True or False

6. compile the Blueprint

7. It means that only the Blueprint that the variable belongs to is allowed to access the variable.

8. 2

9. reusability, editability, reliability, readability

10. Branch Node

11. Select the Actor in the Level Editor, then open the Node Menu in the Blueprint Editor and select "Get reference to [Actor]" near the top of the menu.

12. Select the Actor, then in the Details Panel, click on the blue "Blueprint/Add Script" button.

13. Timeline Node

6

Players & Input

6.1 Game Modes

A *Game Mode* is an Actor that can be used to define and enforce the game's set of rules. These rules may include how many lives the player starts with, whether or not the game can be paused, if there are any time limits, the conditions needed to win the game, and so on. The Game Mode can be set on a per-level basis and you can use the same Game Mode for multiple Levels. In fact, the primary purpose of a Game Mode is to store data and logic that applies to more than one Level and thus isn't appropriate for a Level Blueprint.

To use the Game Mode Actor, you will want to create a Blueprint Class from it. Just like with any other Blueprint, you can create variables to store data, and Nodes to add functionality. For example, you could create an Integer variable called "Start Time" that specifies the amount of seconds that the game timer should start with, and you could use the Event Graph to define how a player wins the game and what should happen when they do.

Create a New Game Mode Blueprint

To create a new Blueprint Class from the Game Mode Actor, go to the Content Browser and browse to the folder you want to put the Blueprint in. Then click the green Add New button and select Blueprint Class.

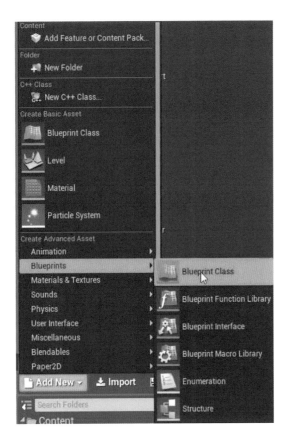

Figure 6.1.1 – Creating a new Blueprint Class

This will open a window where you can choose the parent class you want to derive the new Blueprint from. At the top, there is a list of commonly selected parent classes, and below that is a searchable list of all the classes that can be used. In the list of common classes, click on the Game Mode button. To edit the Blueprint, simply double-click on it to open it in the Blueprint Editor.

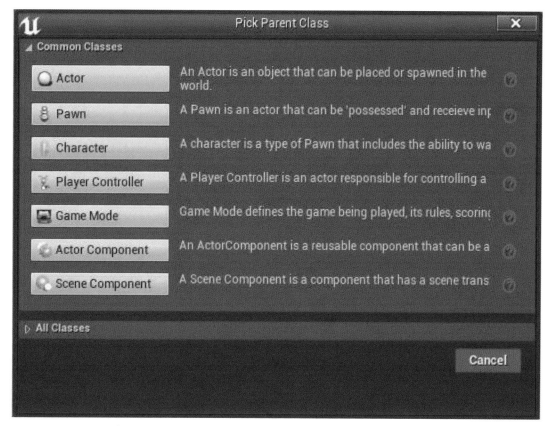

Figure 6.1.2 – Selecting a parent class for the Blueprint Class

Game Mode Properties

The Game Mode class comes with some default properties that can be edited in the Details Panel of the Blueprint Editor.

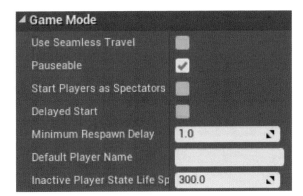

Figure 6.1.3 – Game Mode properties

The first property is *Use Seamless Travel*. This has to do with how players transition between Levels in multiplayer games. With this unchecked, players will disconnect from the server while a new Level loads, and then reconnect to the server once the Level has loaded. With Seamless Travel enabled, the new Level will load in the background and there is no disruption in the server connection. For multiplayer games in Unreal Engine, using Seamless Travel is recommended.

The next property, *Pauseable*, simply determines whether or not the game is allowed to be paused.

The next property is *Start Players as Spectators*. With this unchecked, players will spawn into the game as soon as they connect to the server. With this checked, players who connect to the server will start as Spectators and must spawn into the game manually.

The next property is *Delayed Start*. With this unchecked, the game will begin as soon as the first player connects to the server. With this checked, you must manually script the condition that would cause the game to start.

The property *Minimum Respawn Delay* specifies the minimum amount of time, in seconds, a player must wait to respawn after dying.

Default Player Name will assign a default name to any players who connect to the server with no name specified.

Inactive Player State Life Span specifies the amount of time, in seconds, that a player's data will be kept on the server after they log out. This gives players who disconnect a window where they can still reconnect without being kicked from the game.

Start With Tick Enabled determines if the game will start with the Tick Function enabled, which is something that will fire the Event Tick Node at a specified interval. With the Tick Interval at zero, which is the default, the tick will occur before each frame of gameplay. If an interval is specified, each tick will occur that many seconds from each other. So if a value of 5 is entered, the Event Tick node will fire every five seconds instead of before every frame.

The properties under the Classes category define various gameplay classes that your game will use. For example, the *Default Pawn Class* specifies the Actor that the Player will start off controlling in the game. The *HUD Class* defines what kinds of text overlays you will have during gameplay such as health, lives, score, timer, etc.

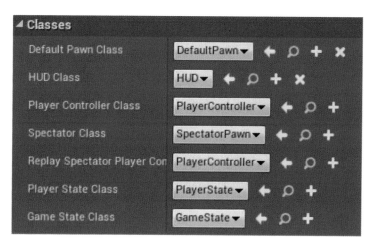

Figure 6.1.4 – You can set game defaults in the Game Mode

There are already defaults for each of the classes. But if you wanted to change, for example, the HUD that a Game Mode used, you could create a new HUD Blueprint Class, and once you saved it, you would be able to select it from the dropdown, telling the Game Mode to use that HUD and not the default.

Assigning Game Modes

After you create a Game Mode Blueprint, you still need to tell the Engine you want to use it. One option you have is to assign it as the default Game Mode for the game that all the Levels will use by default, unless otherwise specified.

To set the default Game Mode, go up to the Menu Bar, click on Edit, and then Project Settings. Then select Maps & Modes from the list on the left. On the screen that comes up, there will be a Default GameMode property that you can set.

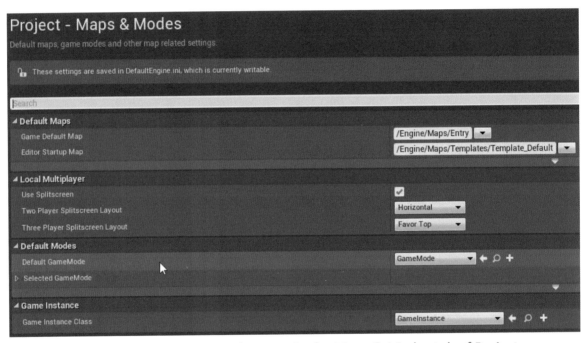

Figure 6.1.5 – You set the Game Mode to use in the Maps & Modes tab of Project Settings

You can also choose to override the default Game Mode on a per-level basis. First, with the Level open that you want to use a different Game Mode for, go up to the Toolbar and click on Settings, and then World Settings. This will open the World Settings tab within the Details Panel. On this tab, there is a property called *GameMode Override*. By default, this is None, which means the Level will use the Default GameMode. But you can choose to override the default by assigning another GameMode using the dropdown.

Figure 6.1.6 – Opening the World Settings tab

Figure 6.1.7 – A GameMode Override can be set in the World Settings tab of the Details Panel

6.2 Pawns

A *Pawn* is an Actor that can be controlled, either by a human player or the computer. Pawns are used for the Actor that you play as in the game and also for AI-controlled allies and enemies.

As you saw in the previous section on Game Modes, the default Game Mode starts with a default Pawn Actor. You've probably already used this Pawn to fly around your practice Levels, even though you can't see it because 1.) it doesn't have a static mesh defined and 2.) the camera is attached to it in a first-person perspective.

You can, however, create your own Pawn Actors, by creating a new Blueprint Class out of the existing Pawn class. Then you would assign the new Pawn as the Default Pawn Class in the Game Mode. To create a new Pawn class, first go to the Content Browser and navigate to the folder you want the Blueprint to be created in. Then click Add New, hover over Blueprints, and select Blueprint Class. Then select the Pawn class as the Parent Class for the Blueprint. To edit the Blueprint, double-click on it to open it in the Blueprint Editor.

In the Viewport tab of the Blueprint Editor, you will see that the Actor starts out consisting of just a single component, the *DefaultSceneRoot* component. This is an advanced topic, so don't worry about what the DefaultSceneRoot is, just know that every Pawn will have one.

Adding a Static Mesh Component to a Pawn

The first thing you may want to consider adding to your Pawn is a Static Mesh Component, so that the Pawn actually looks like something and isn't invisible. To do so, simply click Add Component and select Static Mesh.

Figure 6.2.1 – Adding a Static Mesh Component to an Actor

This will add a Static Mesh Component, but you will still need to define which Static Mesh the component should use. To do that, go to the Static Mesh category of the Details Panel and select one using the dropdown.

Adding a Camera Component to a Pawn

If you are using a Pawn for a human player, you will want to add a *Camera Component* to it, in order to define the perspective that the player will see from. To do so, click Add Component, go down to the Camera category, and select Camera.

Wherever you place the lens of the Camera icon is where the player will see out of. So if you wanted a first-person perspective, you would place the Camera so that the lens was located at the same place as where the Mesh's eyes are supposed to be. Or you could position the Camera elsewhere and have it pointing at the Mesh in order to give it a third-person perspective.

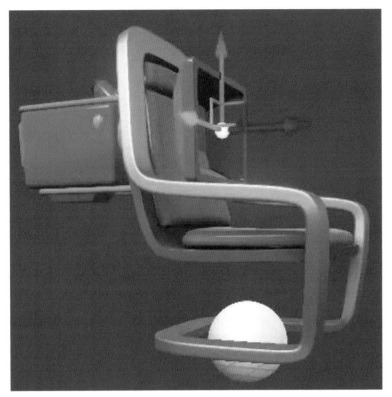

Figure 6.2.2 – This Pawn has a chair for its Mesh. If the chair had eyes in its front, this Camera placement would give a first-person perspective.

Adding a Spring Arm Component to a Pawn

When you are setting up a third-person perspective, you will also want to use a *Spring Arm Component*. The Spring Arm Component will allow the Camera to automatically make adjustments in cases where the line of sight between the Camera and the mesh gets obscured. The Spring Arm Component can also be found under the Camera category.

You will need to attach the Camera to the Spring Arm in order for it to be of use. To do that, select the Camera Component in the Components window, and drag it onto the Spring Arm Component. Once the Camera is attached, you can't use the Move Tool to move it around. At that point, if you want to adjust how far away the Camera is positioned, you will need to set the Target Arm Length property of the Spring Arm, which sets the default length of the Spring Arm.

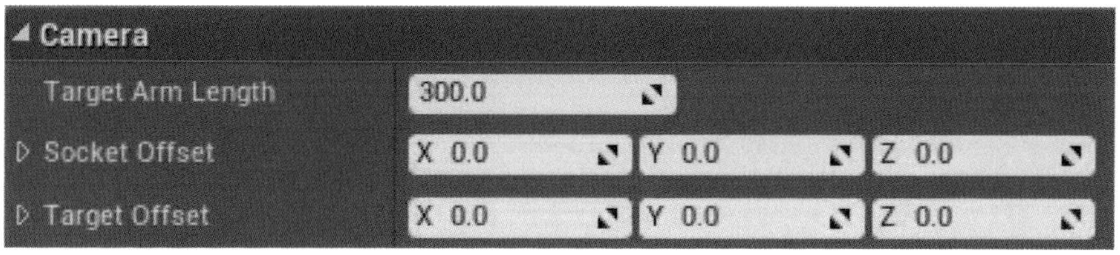

Figure 6.2.3 – Properties of the Spring Arm Component

The Camera will normally be the default length away from the Mesh, but that could change if the Spring Arm needs to adjust because the view of the Camera gets blocked. For example, if a wall gets between the Camera and the Mesh, the Spring Arm will automatically shorten in order to bring the Camera in close enough to be able to see the Mesh again. Then, when the wall was no longer an issue, the Spring Arm would lengthen back to the Target Arm Length.

6.3 Characters

A *Character* is a type of Pawn that has all the features and functionality of a Pawn, plus additional ones. Specifically, a Character is a type of Pawn that is meant to have bipedal movement. Bipedal refers to walking on two legs, so you would use the Character class to represent humans and other creatures with human-like movement, like walking and jumping.

You can create your own Character class the same way as the Game Mode and Pawn class. Go to the Content Browser, go to Add New, select Blueprint Class, and select Character as the Parent Class. As always, double-click it to open it in the Blueprint Editor.

Don't forget to assign your new Character as the Default Pawn Class in the Game Mode. Remember that a Character is a type of Pawn. The Character class is a child of the Pawn class. So the Default Pawn Class can be set to a Pawn class or any child of a Pawn class.

Character Components

The Character class comes with a few different Components. The *Capsule Component* is used as the boundaries of the Character for the purposes of detecting collisions.

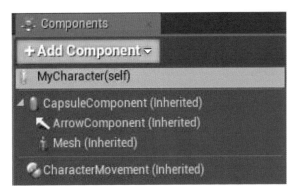

Figure 6.3.1 – The default Components of a Character

The *Arrow Component* is used to indicate which direction should be considered facing-forward for the Character. So if you had a Mesh of a human, you would want the arrow to be coming straight out of the front of its body.

The *Skeletal Mesh Component* can be used to assign a Skeletal Mesh to the Character.

Character Movement Component

Perhaps the most important component of the Character is the *Character Movement Component*. This is what gives the Character its movement capabilities. If you click on it, you can edit several properties relating to its movement.

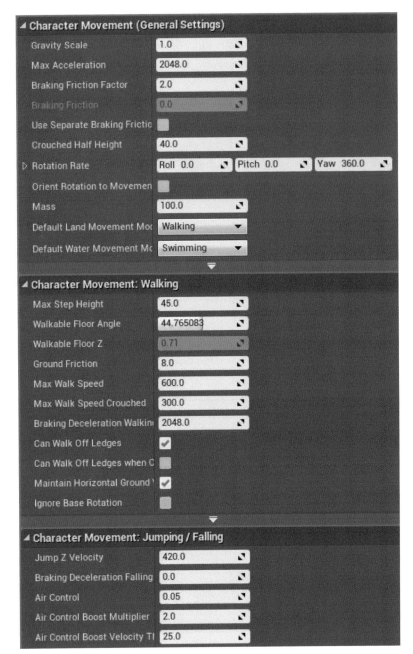

Figure 6.3.2 — Character Movement properties

The *Gravity Scale* property determines how much of an effect gravity will have on this Character. *Max Acceleration* determines the maximum acceleration that this Character can achieve for any type of movement, whether it be walking, swimming, etc. *Braking*

Friction Factor determines how much the Character will glide when attempting to slow down its speed.

The *Mass* property will set the mass of the Character which determines things like how much force is required to move it, and so on. *Max Step Height* determines how tall a step has to be before the Character can no longer automatically ascend it when walking. *Walkable Floor Angle* determines how steep a sloped floor can be before a Character can no longer walk up it.

You can set the Character's maximum walk speed and the max walk speed when the Character is crouched. You can set whether a Character will walk off a ledge when they reach the end of it or if that will block the Character's movement.

There are several properties relating to jumping and falling, such as the *Jump Z Velocity* which will determine how high your Character can jump, and the *Air Control* property which determines how much control you have over your Character when it is in the air. There are also some properties for swimming, flying, and so on.

Creating a Jump Input

The Jump function, as its name implies, will cause your Character to jump. The Jump function is one of many movement functions available to the Character class that is not available to the regular Pawn class.

Adding the following to the Event Graph of the Character Blueprint will cause the Character to jump when the *Space Bar* is pressed:

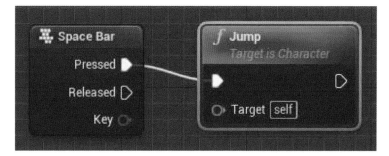

Figure 6.3.3 – Pressing the Space Bar will cause the Character to jump

6.4 Controllers

A *Controller* is an Actor that is used to possess a Pawn and control its movement and actions. There are two types of Controllers - the *Player Controller*, which is used to take input from a human and use that to control a Pawn, and the *AI Controller,* which is used to implement AI control over a Pawn.

You can create a Player Controller Blueprint by creating a new Blueprint Class and using Player Controller as the Parent Class. To use it, you will need to set it as the Player Controller Class in the Game Mode Blueprint.

Figure 6.4.1 – Setting the Player Controller Class in the Game Mode

Advantages of Using a Controller

As you learned in the last section, you can define the input for a Pawn directly in its own Blueprint. But imagine if your game consisted of dozens or even hundreds of characters that the player could control and they all shared many of the same movements. For example, think of the Lego games, like Lego Star Wars, which have dozens of characters you can switch between.

If you were defining the input inside the Pawn, you would have to define it over and over again for each and every Pawn. Then, if you wanted to make even a small change, you would have to make that same change over and over again.

By defining your input inside of a Player Controller instead, you only need to define it in one place, and if you ever need to make a change, you only need to make the change in one place. Then you would be able to use that input on any Pawn that the Player Controller possesses.

Adding Input to a Player Controller

If you tried to add jump functionality, like was done in the previous section, to a Player Controller Blueprint immediately, you won't be able to because the Jump function belongs to the Character class. The Jump Node won't even be available as a selection in the Node Menu.

You would first need to get access to the Character so that you can access its Jump function. This can be done with a *Get Player Character* function. This function will return the Character that the specified player is using. Player index 0 is for player 1 and player index 1 is for player 2 and so on. If the Pawn that the player is using is a Character, the Return Value will contain that Character, otherwise it will return a Null value.

If the Return Value pin contains a valid Character, when you drag off the pin and access the Node Menu, the Jump Node will be available because you are in the context of a Character. The following shows an example of adding jump functionality to a Player Controller:

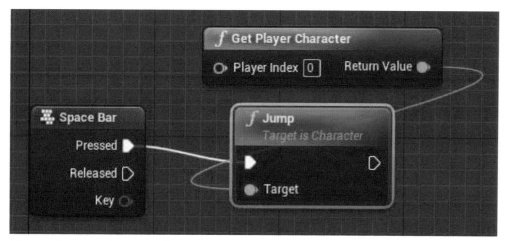

Figure 6.4.2 – The Jump function is only available to the Character class

This provides the same functionality as in the previous example, but now that functionality has been abstracted out to a higher level which will allow you to easily use it with any Character you wish.

6.5 Input Mapping

Imagine you were creating a multiplayer game that could support eight players. You would need eight different Player Controllers - one for each human player that is playing the game. If each Player Controller contained the Jump functionality from the previous section, and you wanted to change what key caused the player to jump from the Space Bar to some other key, you would need to make that change eight times.

But with Input Mapping, you can define what key or keys correspond to what behavior by mapping the keys to a name that you create. Then, you can refer to that name in Player Controller Blueprints instead of hardcoding the specific key to use. If you ever want to change which key corresponds to which action, you will only need to make that change in one place.

Action Mappings vs Axis Mappings

In the Level Editor, go to Edit > Project Settings. Under the Engine category, click on Input. This will bring up the screen where you can create Input Mappings. These are divided into two categories - Action Mappings and Axis Mappings.

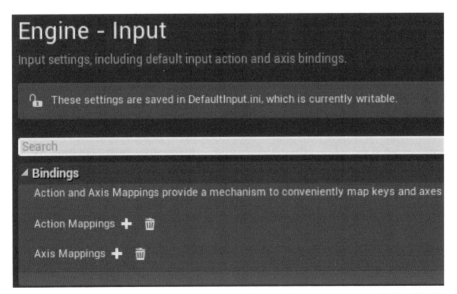

Figure 6.5.1 – You can map inputs in the Engine category of the Project Settings

Action Mappings are for key presses and releases where holding down the key for any length of time doesn't make a difference. For example, if you wanted your character to throw a punch and you wanted the player to have to press a button for each punch, you would use an Action Mapping.

Axis Mappings are used in situations where holding down the key provides a continuous stream of input. For example, you would often use this for walking, where if you hold the key continuously, the character will continue to walk until you let go.

Creating New Input Mappings

To create a new mapping, under the Bindings category, click on the plus sign next to the type of mapping you want to create. If you don't see the new mapping right away, click on the triangle to the left of the label to expand the section.

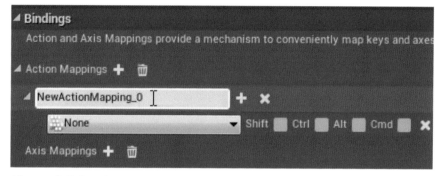

Figure 6.5.2 – Creating a new input mapping

The first box is used to give the mapping a name. Underneath that box is a row where you define a key or button to use that will trigger the action. There are also a series of checkboxes you can check to require that additional keys be held at the same time as the one defined, such as *Shift*, *Ctrl*, or *Alt*.

If you want another key or button to also trigger the same action, just click the plus sign next to the name of the mapping to define another input.

You don't need to save your changes here because any changes made in the Project Settings are automatically saved as they are made. When you are done you can simply close the Project Settings window.

Once you create a mapping, it will be available in the Node Menu and you can use it in place of the keyboard Nodes used in the previous examples:

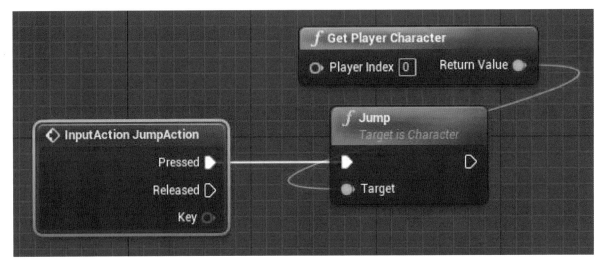

Figure 6.5.3 – Using a mapped action instead of hardcoding the key to use

6.6 Setting Up Basic Character Movement

This section will go through the entire process of setting up basic Character movement. In addition to the jump functionality already covered, you will learn how to move your Character around using the *W*, *A*, *S*, *D* keys, or the left-analog stick of a gamepad, and how to make your Character look around using the mouse or the right-analog stick.

Setting Up the Input Mapping

Go to Edit > Project Settings > Input. Setup an Action Mapping named "JumpAction" like was done in the previous section:

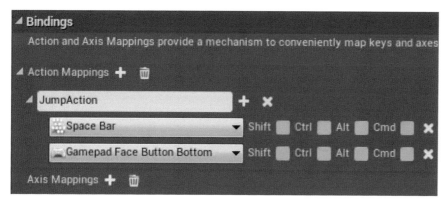

Figure 6.6.1 – Mapping inputs for a jump action

Movement requires detecting a continuous input, so the movement behaviors will use Axis Mappings. Add an Axis Mapping and name it "LookUpDown." To look up and down, we want our player to be able to use either the mouse, by dragging it up or down, or by using the right thumbstick of a gamepad, by tilting it up or down. So click the plus sign to the right of the mapping twice, and select "Mouse Y" for the first input and "Gamepad Right Thumbstick Y-Axis" for the second input.

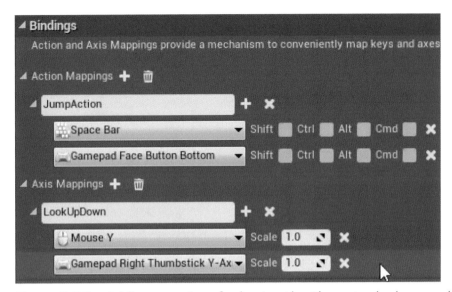

Figure 6.6.2 – Adding mappings for having the Character look around

To the right of the mappings, you will see a *Scale* property. This will determine both the magnitude and direction of the axis input. So if you set the scale of the mouse to 2.0 but left the gamepad at 1.0, then the mouse would cause the player to look up and down twice as fast as using the gamepad.

If you make the Scale negative, it will reverse the direction of the movement applied. With the gamepad scale set at 1.0, tilting the stick up will cause the player to look up and tilting the stick down will cause the player to look down. If it was set to -1.0, it would invert those controls. The mouse Y-axis is inverted by default, so you will need to set that to negative if you want to make it standard.

Continue to add Axis Mappings for the remaining movements until your mappings look like this:

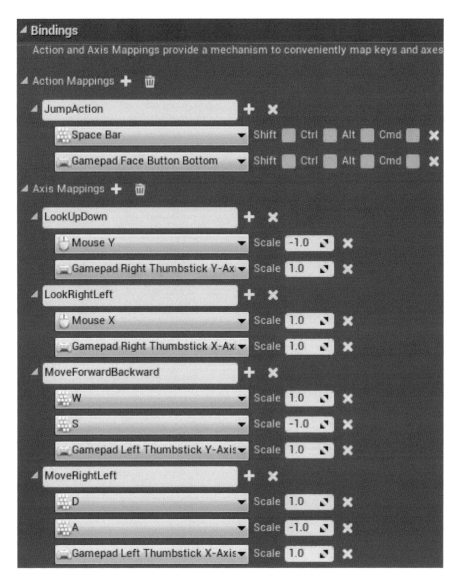

Figure 6.6.3 – Complete input mapping for a Character

Using Input Mappings in Blueprints

Now that you have the input mappings setup, you will need to edit your Player Controller Blueprint so you can specify the behaviors that these mapping names actually correspond to. Before you do that, it will help to place your Character into a variable that you can access it from, so that you don't need to keep calling the Get Player Character function over and over.

So in the Event Graph of the Player Controller Blueprint, add a Get Player Character Node. Drag off the Return Value pin and select *Promote to variable* from the top of the menu. This will create a variable and store the Character in it. In the My Blueprint tab, rename the variable from "NewVar_0" to "MyCharacter."

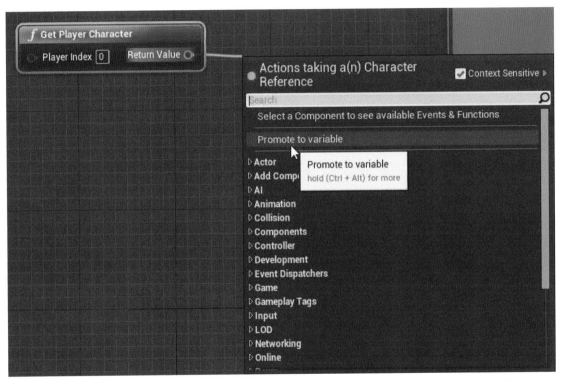

Figure 6.6.4 – Selecting Promote to Variable will create a variable of the same data type as the pin

Connect the output execution pin of the Event BeginPlay Node to the input execution pin of the Set Node. Now, as soon as the Player Controller is created, it will get a reference to the Character and store it in a variable which you can easily access.

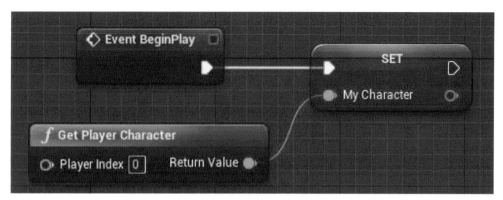

Figure 6.6.5 – This will get a reference to the Character and store it in a variable as soon as the Level begins

Go back to the My Blueprint tab, drag the MyCharacter variable into the Event Graph, and create a Get Node. Drag off the pin of the Get Node and add a Jump Node. Open the Node Menu and search for the "JumpAction" mapping that you created earlier. Add that Node and connect its Pressed pin to the input execution pin of the Jump Node.

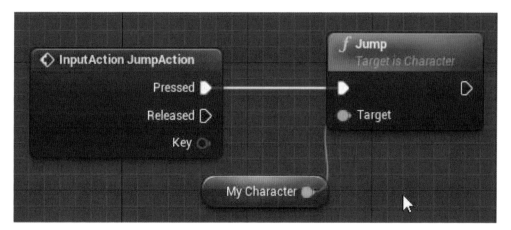

Figure 6.6.6 – The jump logic

Setting Up the Look Movements

In the Node Menu, search for the "LookUpDown" mapping and add that Node. Drag another wire off the MyCharacter node, so you can access the Character's functions, and search for a function called *Add Controller Pitch Input*. The word "pitch" in this context refers to the kind of up and down rotational movement that we're looking to produce.

Connect the output execution pin of the InputAxis LookUpDown Node to the input execution pin of the Add Controller Pitch Input Node. Then take the Axis Value pin of the InputAxis LookUpDown Node, which contains the Scale value you specified in the Input Mappings, and connect it to the Val pin of the Add Controller Pitch Input Node.

Now add the Node for the LookRightLeft mapping you created and connect that to a function called *Add Controller Yaw Input* which is used to control left and right rotational movement. Remember that you need to drag out of the My Character Get Node in order to access Character functions.

Your Event Graph should now look similar to this:

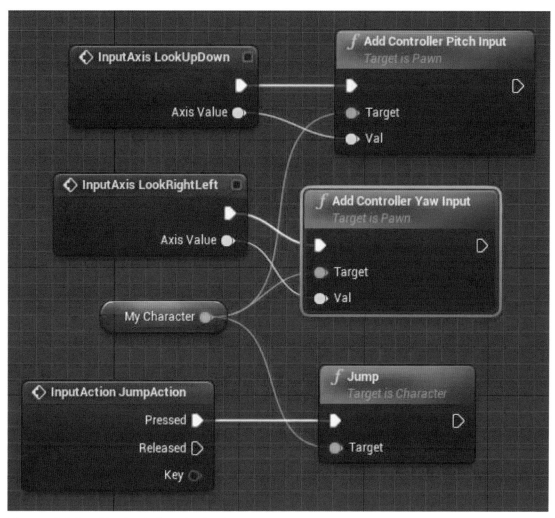

Figure 6.6.7 – The logic for the look movement

There's one more thing you will need to do to get this look functionality working with these functions. Compile and save the Blueprint, and then open your Character Blueprint. In the Details Panel, under the Pawn category, make sure that the two properties *Use Controller Rotation Pitch* and *Use Controller Rotation Yaw* are both checked.

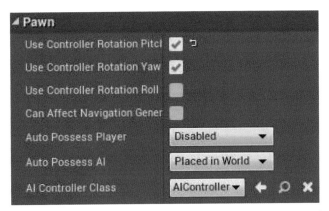

Figure 6.6.8 – Make sure the first two properties here are checked

Setting Up the Walking Movements

Reopen the Player Controller Blueprint. Create another copy of the My Character Get Node to prevent the Event Graph from getting too messy. Add the Node for the MoveForwardBackward mapping and connect that to a function called *Add Movement Input*. Connect the Axis Value pin to the Scale Value pin.

For this to work, you need to provide the Add Movement Input Node with additional information. You need to tell it which direction to move the Character relative to the world. You already know what direction you want to move relative to the character - forward or backward - but which direction is that as far as the Level is concerned? That depends on the direction that the character is facing. So you will need to get the Vector that represents that direction and hook it into the *World Direction* pin.

So drag off the My Character Get Node again, and add the function *Get Control Rotation*. This will tell you how the Character is rotated relative to all three axes. But all you care about at this point is which direction the character is facing. So to get that information, drag off the Return Value pin and add the *Get Forward Vector* function.

This will extract the forward Vector from out of the Rotation value. Now connect the Return Value pin of the Get Forward Vector Node to the World Direction pin of the Add Movement Input Node.

The setup for left and right movement is the same, except you need to use the *Get Right Vector* function instead of the Get Forward Vector function. When you are finished, the logic for the walking movements should look something like this:

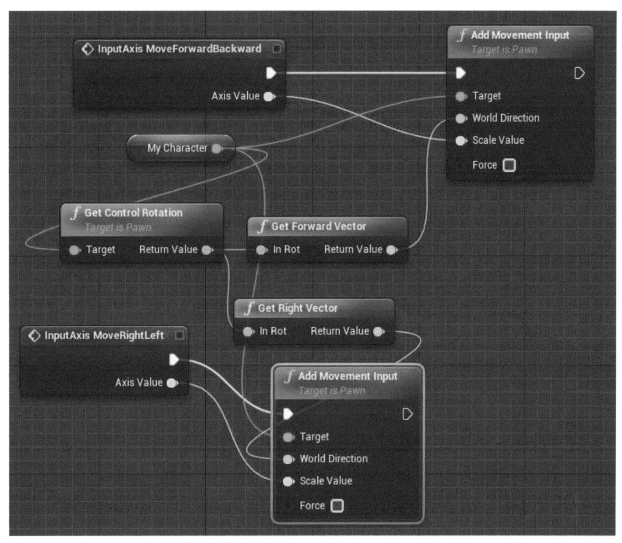

Figure 6.6.9 – The logic for the walking movement

6.7 Chapter 6 Quiz

1. What type of Blueprint Class would you use to store data and logic that applies to multiple Levels?

2. What type of Component, when attached to a camera, will allow the camera to automatically make adjustments in cases where the line of sight between the camera and the mesh gets obscured?

3. What is the parent class of the Character class?

4. Why would you want to define your inputs inside of a Player Controller?

5. What is the difference between Action Mappings and Axis Mappings?

Answers

1. Game Mode

2. Spring Arm Component

3. Pawn

4. Once the input has been defined in a Player Controller, it can easily be applied to any Pawn you want, instead of having to define it over and over in each Pawn. Also, changes only need to be made in one place.

5. Action Mappings are for discrete inputs while Axis Mappings are for continuous inputs.

7

Collisions

7.1 Collisions Overview

In the Details Panel, under the Collision category, you can edit the Collision properties of an Actor.

Hit Events & Overlap Events

If two Actors are set to block one another when they come into contact, then, when they collide, this will generate a *Hit Event* if Hit Events are enabled for that Actor.

To enable Hit Events for an Actor, check the *Simulation Generates Hit Events* checkbox under the Collision category. For an Actor's Hit Event to fire, only the Simulation Generates Hit Events checkbox for that Actor needs to be checked. The other Actor's checkbox only needs to be checked if you want that Actor's Hit Event to fire as well.

Figure 7.1.1 – To enable Hit Events for an Actor, check the Simulation Generates Hit Events checkbox

On the other hand, if two Actors are set to *overlap* with one another, then, when they overlap, this will generate an *Overlap Event* if Overlap Events are enabled for *both* of the Actors.

To enable Overlap Events for an Actor, check the *Generate Overlap Events* checkbox under the Collision category. Again, for an Actor's Overlap Event to fire, both the Actors involved in the collision must have Generate Overlap Events checked.

Hit Events and Overlap Events can be used like any other Event Node and thus can be used to define what should happen when a collision occurs.

Collision Presets

When you expand the menu under the Collision Presets property, you will find a long list of collision properties that can be automatically set by choosing from a list of presets. Or they can be individually set by choosing "Custom" and setting them one-by-one.

Collision Enabled Property

The *Collision Enabled* property is another way to set the block and/or overlap behaviors of the Actor. This has four possible settings. When this is set to *Collision Enabled*, it means that the Actor is enabled for both *Query Collisions* and *Physics Collisions*. Query Collisions just refer to overlap collisions and Physics Collisions refer to blocking collisions.

Figure 7.1.2 – The Collision Enabled property

With Collision Enabled set to *Physics Only*, the Actor will be able to block other Actors, and fire Hit Events, but it won't be able to fire Overlap Events. If it is set to *Query Only*, the Actor will be able to fire Overlap Events but won't be able to block other Actors and won't be able to fire Hit Events. If it is set to *No Collision*, the Actor won't be able to block other Actors and won't be able to fire Overlap Events or Hit Events.

Object Type Property

If the Actor is a Pawn or a Pawn sub-type, such as a Character, you would set the *Object Type* to Pawn. If the Actor is a Vehicle, you would set the Object Type to Vehicle. If the Actor is a Destructible Mesh, a topic that hasn't been covered, you would set it to Destructible.

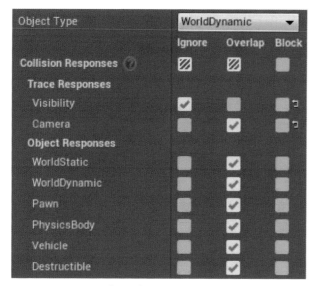

Figure 7.1.3 – The Object Type property and Collision Responses

For all other Actors, if the Actor doesn't move, you would set the Object Type to *WorldStatic*. If the Actor does move, you would set it to either *WorldDynamic* or *PhysicsBody*. You would use WorldDynamic for Actors that move due to an animation or a Blueprint script and PhysicsBody for Actors that will move due to physics, such as gravity or the force of another object.

The Object Type doesn't do anything itself inherently. Its purpose is simply to be able to place each Actor into a specific group, so that you can use the section below it to specify how the different types should interact with each other when they collide.

This section has a row for each of the six Object Types. Each row is used to specify the behavior that should occur when the Actor collides with the Object Type of that row. You can set each row to either *Ignore*, *Overlap*, or *Block*. The first row of checkboxes, labeled *Collision Responses*, can be used as a "select all" for each column. For example, if you click on the Overlap checkbox, it will check the Overlap box in every row.

So if you wanted blocking and Hit Events to occur when the Actor collides with an Actor of the type WorldDynamic, you would check the Block column of the WorldDynamic row. If you wanted the two Actors to overlap and to generate Overlap Events, you would check the box in the Overlap column instead. If you wanted the two Actors to overlap, but not generate any Overlap Events, you would check the Ignore checkbox.

Note that the behavior that will actually occur depends on the above settings for *both* the Actors involved in the collision. For example, both Actors must be set to block the other's type in order for blocking to actually occur and for Hit Events to fire. Similarly, if one of the Actors is set to Ignore the other, then Overlap Events won't fire even if the other Actor is set to Overlap.

Trace Responses

The Trace Responses section is used to determine the Actor's visibility to other Actors. If the Actor doing the looking is a camera, you would use the Camera row, and for all other Actor types, you would use the Visibility row.

If the Actor is set to Ignore, it will be invisible to other Actors. If it is set to Overlap, it can be seen by other Actors, but it can also be seen through. So you would use this for a glass wall, for example. If it is set to Block, then it can be seen, but it cannot be seen through. So you might use this for a brick wall, for example.

Collision Preset Property

Again, if you want to be able to set the above properties manually, you need to set the Collision Preset to Custom. But you can also use the dropdown to select from a long list of presets. Each preset will automatically select some combination of the properties.

For example, with *BlockAll* as the preset, it will automatically set the Collision Enabled property to Collision Enabled, it will set the Object Type to WorldStatic, and it will set all of the responses to Block. If *OverlapAll* is selected, it will set Collision Enabled to Query Only, it will set the Object Type to WorldStatic, and it will set all of the responses to Overlap. If *OverlapAllDynamic* is selected, it will choose the same settings as OverlapAll, except it will set the Object Type to WorldDynamic.

Can Character Step Up On Property

The *Can Character Step Up On* property is used to specify whether or not a Character will step onto the top of the Actor when it walks into it or if it will block the Character's movement. This is assuming that the two Actors' Object Types are set to Block one another. Otherwise, this property doesn't apply. Also, at very small heights, a Character will step onto an Actor when it walks into it regardless of what this property is set to.

Figure 7.1.4 – The Can Character Step Up On property

So if the Actor is tall enough, with Can Character Step Up On set to *ECB No*, if a Character walks into the Actor, it will block the Character's movement. But if it is set to *ECB Yes*, when a Character walks into the Actor, it will step *onto* the Actor instead.

If Can Character Step Up On is set to *ECB Owner*, then the Actor will use the same setting as its parent. If it doesn't have a parent, then setting this to ECB Owner is the same as setting it to ECB Yes.

7.2 Causing Damage Due to Collisions

This section will demonstrate a practical use for collisions by showing you how you could deduct health from a Character when it collides with an enemy or some harmful object. Before we get to the example, however, there are two more Nodes you should be familiar with – the Event Hit Node and the Apply Damage Node.

Event Hit Node

An *Event Hit Node,* inside an Actor's Blueprint, will fire any time that Actor registers a Hit Event. The Node contains several output pins.

Figure 7.2.1 – The Event Hit Node

The *My Comp* pin will return which Component of this Actor was hit. The *Other* pin will return the other Actor that collided with this Actor. The *Other Comp* pin will return the Component of the other Actor that was hit.

The *Self Moved* pin is a Boolean that will tell you if the collision was directly caused by the player. If the player collides with the Actor, or if a projectile fired from the player collides with the Actor, this will return False. For any other collisions, this will return True.

The *Hit Location* pin is a Vector value that will return the X, Y, and Z coordinates of the location where the hit occurred. The *Hit Normal* pin is a Vector value that will return the direction of the impact. So it will return the angles relative to the X, Y, and Z axes. The *Normal Impulse* pin will return how much force the impact had in the X, Y, and Z directions.

The *Hit* pin contains even more data about the collision. If you drag off the pin and select "Break Hit Result", it will create a *Break Hit Result Node* containing many more details about the collision should you need to access that information.

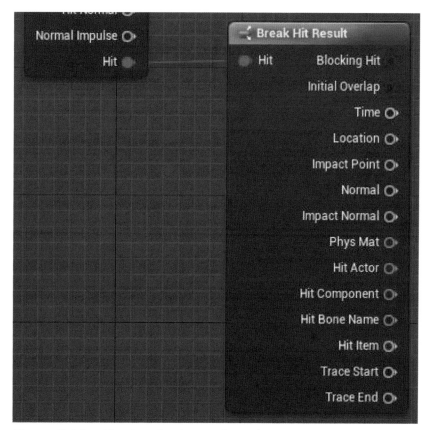

Figure 7.2.2 – The Break Hit Result Node

Apply Damage Node

The *Apply Damage Node* will activate a *Damage Event* for whatever Actor is passed into its *Damaged Actor* pin. The Apply Damage Node will also pass the data from its other pins to the Damage Event. It is then up to the Actor receiving the Damage to define in its Blueprint how it should handle that incoming information.

Figure 7.2.3 – The Apply Damage Node

The *Base Damage* pin is used to specify how much Damage should be applied. So you would specify higher Base Damages for Actors that should be more powerful or harmful. Note that this value is arbitrary until you give it some meaning with further logic.

Imagine that the Damage is supposed to be the result of a Character firing a projectile and hitting an Actor with that projectile. In that situation, the Character who fired the projectile would be considered the *Event Instigator* and the projectile itself would be considered the *Damage Causer*. So if you needed to pass that information into the Damage Event, you would use those pins.

Using a *Damage Type Class* is optional, but if you want, you could create Blueprints that specify different types of Damage, and then use this pin to specify which type of Damage this is supposed to be.

Damage Example

In this example, we will use a Cube Mesh to represent an enemy or some sort of object that would cause harm upon contact. The cube's Simulation Generates Hit Events property has been checked and it is set to block all other Actor types.

The cube has been converted into a Blueprint Class by clicking on the blue "Blueprint/Add Script" button in the Details Panel. In the cube's Blueprint, an Event Hit Node has been added that will cause an Apply Damage Node to fire. The Other pin of the Event Hit Node has been connected to the Damaged Actor pin of the Apply Damage Node, meaning that whatever Actor collides with the cube will register a Damage Event.

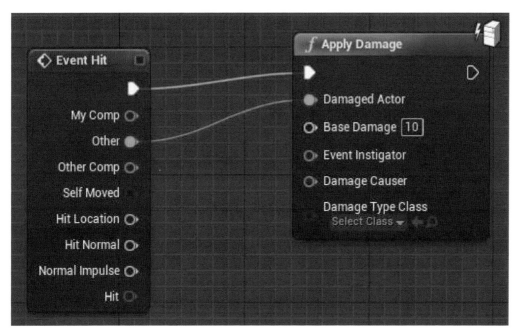

Figure 7.2.4 – The logic in this Cube's Blueprint will cause Damage to be applied to any Actor that collides with it

In the Character Blueprint, a Float variable named "Health" has been added and given a default value of 100. An *Event AnyDamage Node* has been added that will fire any time the Character registers a Damage Event. The Event AnyDamage Node will trigger a Set Node that will set the Health variable to whatever its current value is minus the amount of Damage received in the Damage Event. This calculation is performed by a *Float Minus Float Node*.

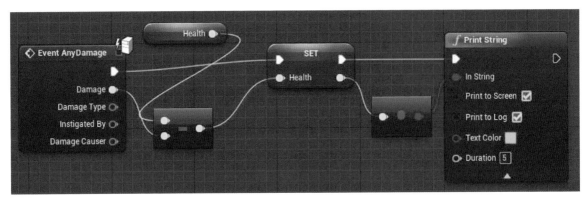

Figure 7.2.5 – When this Character takes Damage, the value of that Damage will be subtracted from the Character's Health variable

After the new value of the Health variable is set, a Print String Node will print this value to the screen so the player can see how much health the Character has remaining. When connecting the pin containing the value of the variable to the In String pin, a Node was automatically created in-between to convert the data from a Float to a String.

However, there is still a slight problem with this example. If the Character runs into the cube even for a half-second and the game is running at thirty frames per second, that means that the Event Hit node is going to fire fifteen times, because that is the number of frames of gameplay that is occurring during that half-second. With the current logic, this will cause the Character to get health deducted fifteen times.

Making a Character Temporarily Invincible

The solution is to make your Character temporarily invincible after every time they receive Damage. You've probably noticed in several games that when your Character takes damage, there is a split-second where they are immune to additional damage. This is to get around this problem of the game registering multiple collisions for what you and I would think of as just a single collision.

This can be accomplished by using a DoOnce Node and a Delay Node in the following manner:

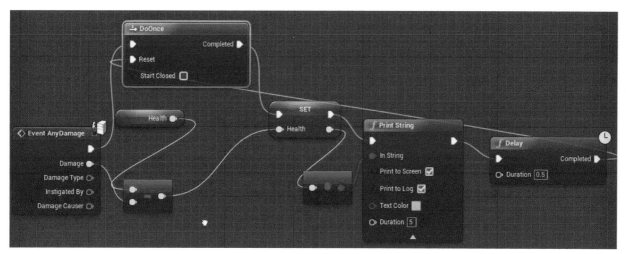

Figure 7.2.6 – This will make the Character invincible for a half-second after it takes Damage

Now when the Character takes Damage, after it deducts the Damage from the health and prints the health to the screen, there will be a half-second delay during which the DoOnce Node will be closed. Any Damage Events that fire during that half-second will be blocked by the closed DoOnce Node. Then, after the half-second has expired, the DoOnce Node will get reset, and Damage Events will once again affect the Character.

Destroying a Character

The following logic can be added to the above example to destroy the Character once the Character's Health reaches zero:

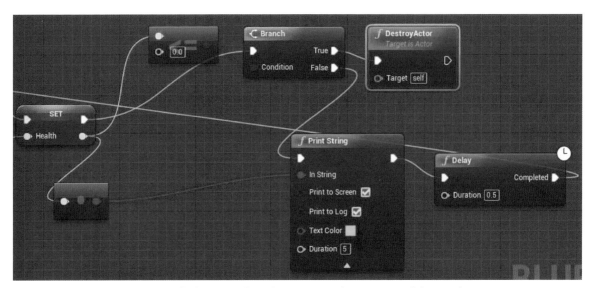

Figure 7.2.7 – This logic will destroy the Character when its Health reaches zero

Instead of going straight to the Print String Node after setting the new Health value, the Blueprint will first check to see if the Health has reached zero yet. It does this by using a *Float Less-Than-Or-Equal-To Float Node* that will look at the Float value in its first input pin and tell you if that value is less than or equal to the Float value in its second input pin.

If the Health variable is less than or equal to zero, the Branch Node will route execution to a *DestroyActor Node* which will destroy the Actor in its Target pin. Otherwise, the Branch Node will route execution to the Print String Node as before.

7.3 Chapter 7 Quiz

1. If two Actors are set to Block one another's type, and the Simulation Generates Hit Events property is True for Actor 1 and False for Actor 2, when they collide, will Actor 1 register a Hit Event?

2. If two Actors are set to Overlap one another's type, and the Generate Overlap Events property is True for Actor 1 and False for Actor 2, when they overlap, will Actor 1 register an Overlap Event?

3. What do Query Collisions and Physics Collisions refer to?

4. If an Actor doesn't move, what should you set its Object Type to?

5. What should you set the Trace Responses to for a Static Mesh Actor meant to represent a transparent glass wall?

6. What does an Apply Damage Node do?

7. In a general sense, what is the strategy to prevent an Actor from registering too many Damage Events when colliding with something the applies Damage to it?

Answers

1. Yes. For an Actor's Hit Event to fire, only the Simulation Generates Hit Events property for that Actor needs to be True.

2. No. For an Actor's Overlap Event to fire, both the Actors involved must have their Generate Overlap Events property set to True.

3. Query Collisions refer to overlap collisions and Physics Collisions refer to blocking collisions.

4. WorldStatic

5. Overlap. This means other Actors will be able to register that the wall is there and also be able to detect Actors that are behind the wall.

6. An Apply Damage Node will activate a Damage Event for the Actor connected to its Damaged Actor pin. It will also pass the data from its other pins to the Damage Event.

7. Make that Actor temporarily immune to Damage for a short time after each Damage Event.

8

User Interfaces ◆

8.1 UMG Overview

In this chapter, you will learn how to create user interfaces for your game, such as menus and HUDs. *Menus* are used when the player needs to make a choice from a list, such as choosing between "Start New," "Continue," and "Options" at the beginning of a game.

HUD stands for "Heads Up Display." This is the information that is displayed to the player while the game is in progress. For example, health, ammo, score, time remaining, etc.

History of Unreal Interfaces

There are a few different ways to create menus and HUDs in Unreal Engine. The original way was to create a HUD Blueprint. Then, you would script the User Interface elements in this Blueprint, and then go into the Game Mode and set that HUD Blueprint as the default for the Game Mode.

This method is outdated, but it is covered here so that if you run across a HUD Blueprint, you know what it is, and also so you don't wonder why we aren't setting the HUD Class in the Game Mode like we are the other classes.

In Unreal Engine 3, Epic Games released the *Slate* framework, which was an improved method for creating UI elements, but one that was still pure scripting.

Finally, in Unreal Engine 4, they built a framework on top of Slate called Unreal Motion Graphics, or *UMG* for short. What's great about UMG is that it's a visual system for creating UI elements. This makes it much quicker to create your layouts and much easier to see what the result will be.

Widget Blueprints

To use UMG, you will first need to create a *Widget Blueprint*. A Widget Blueprint is where you will design the layout you want to use for your HUD, menu, etc. If you're not familiar with the term widget - in the context of computing, the definition of a widget is "a component that enables a user to perform a function." That's basically what a widget is in UMG. For example, you might create a menu widget that enables a user to choose from a list of options.

Another thing you should know about widgets in UMG is that widgets can, and often do, contain other widgets. For example, a menu widget would probably be made up of multiple button widgets. And then the menu widget itself could be placed inside another menu widget as a sub-menu, and so on.

To create a Widget Blueprint, go to the Content Browser, click the "Add New" button, scroll down to "User Interface," and select "Widget Blueprint."

Figure 8.1.1 – Adding a new Widget Blueprint

In order for a widget to appear in-game, it will need to be called from another Blueprint, such as the Level Blueprint or the Blueprint of a Pawn. The following is an example of calling a widget named "My Widget" from a Character Blueprint:

Figure 8.1.2 – This logic renders a Widget Blueprint named "My Widget" in memory and adds it to the screen

The *Create Widget Node* will create a copy of the widget specified in its *Class* pin. The *Owning Player* pin specifies the Player Controller that the widget should be applied to. If nothing is connected, it will be applied to the default Player Controller.

The *Add to Viewport Node* will display the widget passed into its Target pin on the screen. When you want to remove a widget from the Viewport, you need to use the *Remove From Parent Node*, and connect the widget you want removed to that Node's Target pin.

Widget Blueprint Editor

The *Widget Blueprint Editor* is divided into two tabs - the Designer tab, where you construct the interface, and the Graph tab where you can script logic for the interface. You can switch between the two by clicking on their buttons in the upper-right.

Figure 8.1.3 – These buttons are used to switch between the Designer tab and Graph tab

The main window of the Designer tab is the *Visual Designer* in the center. This is where you will create the layouts for your interfaces.

Figure 8.1.4 – The Visual Designer

In the upper-left, is the *Palette* window. This window contains pre-made widgets that you can drag-and-drop into the Visual Designer to construct your layouts.

Figure 8.1.5 – The Palette window

Below that is the *Hierarchy* window. This window is very similar to the World Outliner in the Level Editor. It organizes the elements in the Visual Designer and shows their parent-child relationships.

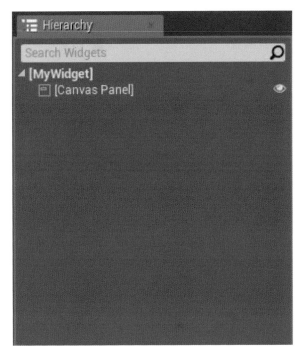

Figure 8.1.6 – The Hierarchy window

To the right of the Visual Designer is the *Details* window. This is just like its counterpart in the Level Editor. When you select one of your widgets, you will be able to view and edit the properties of that widget in the Details window.

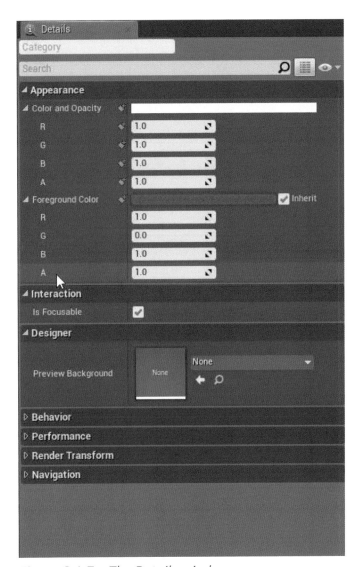

Figure 8.1.7 – The Details window

At the bottom are two windows that can be used to animate your layouts. For example, if you had a menu, you could make it fly in from the edge of the screen or something, if you wanted, instead of it just appearing.

At the top is the *Toolbar*. It contains a Compile button and a Save button, like in other Blueprints. To the right of the Save button is the *Find in Content Browser* button. If you have an element in your layout that came from the Content Browser and not from the

Palette window, you can select that element and click the Find in CB button to be taken to that asset within the Content Browser.

Figure 8.1.8 – The Toolbar

The *Play* button will start a simulation of your game in the Level Editor, just like the Play button in that window will. But the reason there is a Play button here as well, is because whenever your game is being simulated, the UI portion of the game will be simulated in the Visual Designer.

8.2 Root Widget

A Widget Blueprint will always consist of at least a *Root Widget*, which will have the same name as the Widget Blueprint itself. The Root Widget will always be the first element listed in the Hierarchy window.

Whenever you create a new Widget Blueprint, it will, by default, start out with a *Canvas Panel* added as a child of the Root Widget. The Canvas Panel will be covered in detail in the next section, so, for now, just know that it is a container that is used to hold other widgets.

Figure 8.2.1 – The Root Widget of a Widget Blueprint named "MyWidget" with a Canvas Panel child

Color and Opacity

If you select the Root Widget, you can view and edit its properties in the Details window. Starting with the *Appearance* category, you have the Color and Opacity and the Foreground Color properties. Both of these colors can be set either by clicking on the colored strip and using the Color Picker, or by expanding their respective menus and setting the red, green, blue, and alpha settings directly.

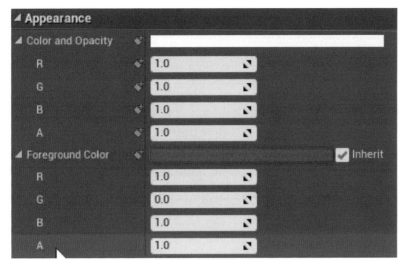

Figure 8.2.2 – The Appearance category for a Root Widget

Whatever color you set the *Color and Opacity* to in the Root Widget will be applied to all child widgets. That color will be combined with the color of the child itself, with the color white being ignored. Here are a few examples to clarify this.

Imagine that a Text Widget has been added as a child of the Canvas Panel. Because the Canvas Panel is a child of the Root Widget, by extension, the Text Widget is now also a child of the Root Widget. If the color of the Root Widget is white, and the color of the Text Widget is blue, then the white will be ignored, and the text will appear blue. Conversely, if the Root Widget is set to blue, and the Text Widget is set to white, the white of the Text Widget will be ignored, and the text will again appear blue.

But now let's say that the Root Widget is set to blue, and the Text Widget is set to yellow. These two colors will combine, and the text will appear green. So again, the Color and Opacity of the Root Widget gets combined with the color of the child, with the color white being ignored.

Foreground Color

The *Foreground Color* property of the Root Widget is similar to the Color and Opacity property, except that it will only be applied to children whose color property is set to *Inherit*. Note that not all color properties have an Inherit property, so you won't be able to apply this to all types of widgets.

If the Color and Opacity of the Root Widget is set to white and the Foreground Color is set to yellow, and the Color and Opacity of the Text Widget is set to red, the text will appear red. But if the Inherit property of the Text Widget is checked, the color of the text changes to yellow, because it is now ignoring the red color and instead inheriting from the next highest color property which is the Foreground Color property of the Root Widget.

Now, if the Color and Opacity of the Root Widget is changed to blue, the text will appear green because the Text Widget is now receiving the blue from the Color and Opacity property and the yellow from the Foreground Color property.

The Foreground Color property of the Root Widget has an Inherit property itself. If this is checked, the color set there will be ignored, and the Foreground Color will instead inherit the color of the Color and Opacity property.

Continuing with the above examples, if the Inherit property of the Foreground Color of the Root Widget was checked at this point, the text will appear blue again, because the Text Widget is inheriting the color of the Root Widget's Foreground Color property, which is in turn inheriting the color of the Root Widget's Color and Opacity property.

Is Focusable

The *Interaction* category contains just one property, *Is Focusable*. If this is checked, the widget will be able to attain *focus*. A widget can attain focus by being clicked on, or navigated to by the keyboard. A widget that has focus will be able to accept input from the keyboard.

Figure 8.2.3 – The Interaction category

For example, if a button has focus, then pressing Enter on the keyboard will cause that button to be pressed. If Is Focusable is unchecked, the widget will not be able to be navigated to, and if it is clicked on, it will still register click events, but it will not take focus away from whatever other widget currently has it.

Background Property

The *Designer* category also contains just one property, *Background*. You can use the dropdown to choose an image, and whatever image you select will be used as the background for the entire widget.

Figure 8.2.4 – The Designer category

8.3 Canvas Panel

Whenever you create a new Widget Blueprint, it will automatically add a *Canvas Panel* to the Root Widget by default. However, you can delete it if you want, and you can manually add Canvas Panels to the layout via the Panel category of the Palette.

In the context of UMG, a *Panel* is a container that is useful for aligning widgets and moving widgets as a group. Each Panel has its own unique type of slot, which gives its children different positioning and sizing capabilities.

For example, when a widget is added to a Canvas Panel, it is placed inside of a *Canvas Panel Slot*. A Canvas Panel Slot allows for absolute positioning, meaning you can specify the exact location you want the widget to be located within the Canvas Panel. If you added a widget to a *Grid Panel*, however, it would go into a *Grid Slot*, and you would specify the widget's location by row and column instead of by exact pixels.

Canvas Panel Slot Properties

You can position a widget inside of a Canvas Panel using the *Position X* and *Position Y* properties. You can size the widget to an exact size using the *Size X* and *Size Y* properties.

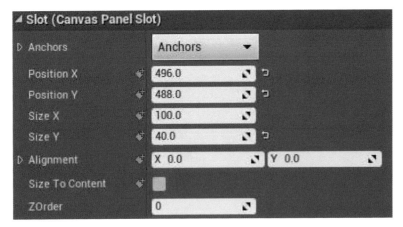

Figure 8.3.1 – The properties of a Canvas Panel Slot

Anchors

Up at the top of the Slot category are *Anchors*. Anchors are a way to specify where on the edge of the Panel the location of a Widget should be measured from, in the scenario that the window size or screen size changes.

An *Anchor Medallion* will appear in the spot where the Slot is anchored. For example, if a button is placed into a slot and anchored to the top-left of the screen, an Anchor Medallion will appear in the top-left corner of the Visual Designer. If you ran the game, no matter how you resized the window, the button would stay in the same position relative to the top-left corner.

Figure 8.3.2 – An Anchor Medallion

By clicking on the Anchors button, you can choose a different location to anchor the widget. You could anchor it to the top-center edge, to the upper-right corner, and so on. There are also six Anchors available that will anchor the widget to two sides of the canvas. The Anchor in the bottom-right of the Anchor Menu will anchor the widget to all four corners of the canvas and stretch and shrink it in all directions as you resize the window.

The coordinate system that the Position X and Position Y properties use is based on where the widget is anchored to. So when a slot is anchored to the top-left, the position (0,0) is located in the top-left. But if the slot were anchored to the top-right, then position (0,0) would be located in the top-right, and so on.

The question of which point on the widget should be used as the Anchor's location is determined by the *Alignment* property. The Alignment property uses a coordinate system where (0,0) represents the top-left corner of the widget, and (1,1) represents the bottom-right.

So if a slot is anchored to the top-left, and its position is set to (0,0), when its Alignment is set to (0,0), its top-left corner will align with the top-left corner of the Canvas.

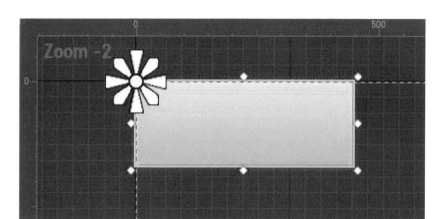

Figure 8.3.3 — A Button Widget anchored to the top-left, at position (0,0) and alignment (0,0)

If the Alignment was changed to (1,1), its bottom-right corner will be aligned with the corner of the Canvas.

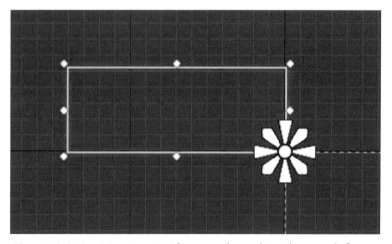

Figure 8.3.4 - A Button Widget anchored to the top-left, at position (0,0) and alignment (1,1)

If it were changed to (0.5,0.5), the center of the slot will be aligned with the corner.

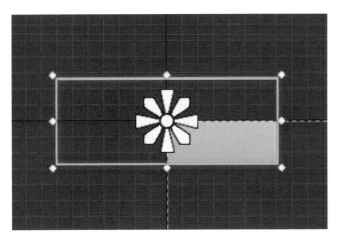

Figure 8.3.5 - A Button Widget anchored to the top-left, at position (0,0) and alignment (0.5,0.5)

Size to Content

Normally, a Text Widget will not resize its box even if the text inside it is too large to hold. In this scenario, you could manually resize the box using the Size X and Size Y properties. But if you want the box to be exactly big enough to show the text inside of it, you can check the *Size to Content* property and it will automatically adjust the size. Note that when the Size to Content property is checked, the Size X and Size Y settings will be ignored.

ZOrder

The *ZOrder* property determines the order in which widgets get drawn to the screen and, thus, for widgets in the same location, determines which widget overlaps which. Lower numbers get drawn first.

If you have a button whose ZOrder is 0, and some text whose ZOrder is 1, then the button will be drawn first, followed by the text. So if these are in the same location, the text will overlap the button since it gets drawn last.

Figure 8.3.6 – A Button Widget with a ZOrder of 0 and a Text Widget with a ZOrder of 1

But if the ZOrder of the button was changed to 2, then the button would now get drawn last and thus appear on top.

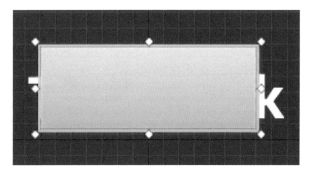

Figure 8.3.7 - A Button Widget with a ZOrder of 2 and a Text Widget with a ZOrder of 1

8.4 Common Widget Properties

There are four categories in the Details Panel that are common to all widgets, and those are Behavior, Performance, Render Transform, and Navigation.

Behavior Category

Starting with the *Behavior* category, the first property is *Is Enabled*. If this is unchecked, it will disable the widget, meaning it cannot be interacted with by the user. So widgets like buttons, checkboxes, sliders, and so on, will not be able to receive input. For example, a disabled button will be a darker shade of grey than an enabled button, and if you click on it, it won't change color like an enabled button because it is not registering the click.

Figure 8.4.1 – The Behavior category

To the right of the Is Enabled property, and several other properties as well, is a dropdown that says *Bind*. You can use this to bind the property that it's next to, to a variable. For example, you could create a Boolean variable and if you bound that to the Is Enabled property for a button, then when that variable were True, the button would be enabled, and when it was False, the button would be disabled. This allows widgets to have properties that can change during run-time if your game logic ends up changing the value of the variable that the property is bound to.

The next property is *Tool Tip Text*. By adding text to this property, it will cause that text to appear whenever the user hovers the mouse over the widget. This is useful for providing further clarity to the user about how to use the widget, or what its purpose is.

The next property is *Visibility*. By default, it is set to *Visible* which means it can be seen by the user, interacted with by the user, and it takes up space in the layout. If a widget is set to *Collapsed*, it will be invisible to the user, it cannot be interacted with by the user, and it won't take up any space in the layout. If a widget is set to *Hidden*, it will be invisible to the user, and cannot be interacted with by the user, but it will take up space in the layout.

A setting of *Hit Test Invisible* is essentially the same as making the widget not focusable and not enabled, with the exception being that its appearance won't change, so it won't be grayed out like a widget normally would be when disabled. The final value is *Self Hit Test Invisible*. This is the same as Hit Test Invisible except that it won't apply to child widgets like the Hit Test Invisible setting will.

Performance Category

The next category, *Performance*, has just one property, *Is Volatile*.

Figure 8.4.2 – The Performance category

The Is Volatile property is used with the *Invalidation Box* widget in the Optimization category of the Palette. The purpose of the Invalidation Box is to cache its children widgets, meaning save them in memory. This will increase performance if those widgets don't change often. But if one of those child widgets does change often, such as one that animates and needs to be drawn differently each frame, you would not want to try to cache that widget. In that scenario, you would set the widget's Is Volatile property to True, to prevent it from being cached.

Render Transform Category

The next category is *Render Transform*. If you expand the *Transform* menu, you will see four properties, Translation, Scale, Shear, and Angle.

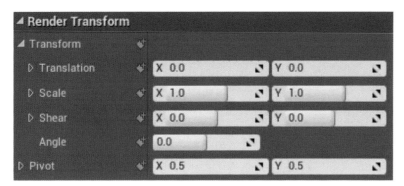

Figure 8.4.3 – The Render Transform category

With the *Translation* property, you can change the location of the widget. With the *Scale* property, you can change the size of the widget. These work very similar to the Position and Size properties inside of a Canvas Panel Slot. But the transform that occurs within a slot is known as a *Layout Transform*, as opposed to a *Render Transform*. The difference is that a Layout Transform can affect and be affected by the other widgets in the layout while a Render Transform will ignore the layout.

For example, imagine there were three buttons in a row, side-by-side, inside a Horizontal Box Panel (Horizontal Box Panels will be covered later in the chapter).

Figure 8.4.4 – Three Button Widgets in a Horizontal Box Panel

If you increased the size of the middle button with a Layout Transform, by adjusting the properties of its Horizontal Box Slot, it would shrink the size of the two buttons beside it.

Figure 8.4.5 – The size of the middle button has been increased via a Layout Transform

Also, the size you could increase the middle button would be limited by the size of the Horizontal Box that it's in. However, if you change its size using a Render Transform, by adjusting the Scale property of the Render Transform category, the other two buttons will be ignored, as will the bounds of the Horizontal Box.

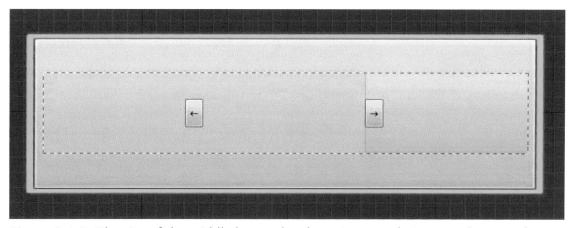

Figure 8.4.6 - The size of the middle button has been increased via a Render Transform

Most of the time, you will want to use Layout Transforms to set the position and size of your widgets, but Render Transforms can be useful in some situations, such as animating your widgets.

The next property is *Shear*. You can use the Shear property to distort the widget diagonally.

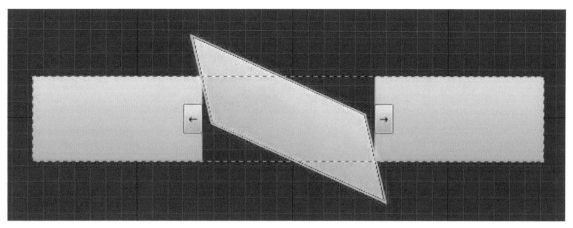

Figure 8.4.7 – The Shear property can be used to skew the shape of widgets

The *Angle* property can be used to rotate the widget.

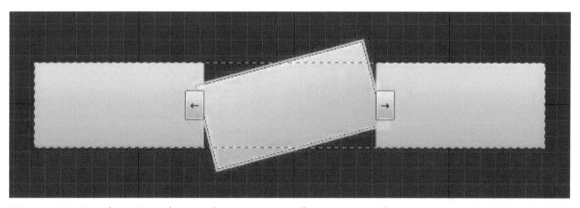

Figure 8.4.8 – Changing the Angle property will rotate a widget

Finally, there is the *Pivot* property. Just like the Alignment property of the Canvas Panel Slot, this uses a coordinate system of (0,0) to indicate the top-left of the widget and (1,1) to indicate the bottom-right of the widget. By default, it is set to (0.5,0.5) which places the pivot point in the center of the widget. So with the pivot point in the center, if you were to, for example, rotate the widget, it would rotate around its center. If you scaled the widget, it would expand outwards from the center and inwards towards the center.

But if you were to change this to (0,0), then the pivot point would now be the top-left corner of the widget. Now if you rotate it, instead of it rotating around its center, it will rotate around its top-left corner. When you scale the widget, it will now expand from the left and the top.

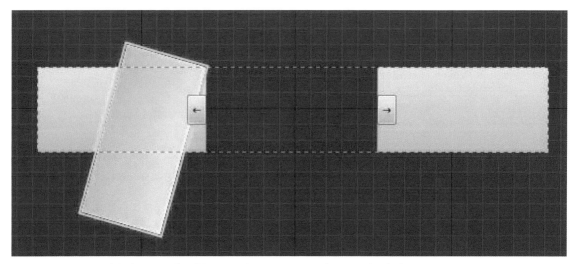

Figure 8.4.9 – This button had its Angle property changed while its Pivot point was set to (0,0)

Navigation Category

The final category is *Navigation*. This category affects how the user can navigate to the different widgets using their keyboard.

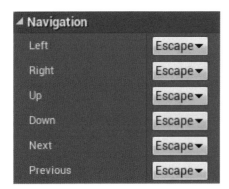

Figure 8.4.10 – The Navigation category

By default, all the properties here are set to *Escape*. Escape basically means that you are able to escape that widget in that direction. For example, if a button's *Left* property is set to Escape, this means that if that button has focus and you press left on the keyboard, focus will move left to the next widget. But if you were to change the Left property to *Stop* instead, then navigation can no longer move to the left through the widget.

The *Wrap* setting can be used with certain Panels, such as a Uniform Grid Panel. This needs to be set on the Panel itself. For example, if you had a Uniform Grid Panel that contained a grid of buttons, and you set its Left and Right navigation properties to Wrap, then when the player pressed left on the keyboard when focused on one of the left-most buttons, focus will wrap around to the first button on the other side, and vice-versa.

By setting the value to *Explicit*, you can specify the widget you want the focus to move to when navigation moves in that direction. Simply type the name of the widget you want focus to move to in the box that appears.

Figure 8.4.11 – When navigating to the right from this widget, focus will move to a widget named "Button2"

8.5 Visual Designer

The *Visual Designer* is the main window of the Designer tab. If you hold down the RMB and drag, you can pan about the window. If you use the scroll wheel on the mouse, you can zoom in and out. In the upper-left corner, it will tell you just how much you are zoomed in or out.

In the upper-right corner, there is a row of buttons that pertain specifically to the Visual Designer. The first pair of buttons is used to toggle between Layout Transform and Render Transform, and you can use the shortcut keys W and E as well.

Figure 8.5.1 – Use these buttons to toggle between Layout Transform and Render Transform

As discussed in the previous section, a Layout Transform is when you adjust the positioning, etc. of a widget within its slot, which causes the widget to be bound by the layout. A Render Transform is when you make those adjustments within the Render Transform category, which causes the widget to ignore the layout.

Note that if you use Render Transform here, it will NOT change the way the sizing control behaves when you click and drag on the edges of a widget, it will still behave like a Layout Transform. So these buttons only affect positioning.

To the right of those buttons are a pair of buttons used to set Grid Snapping. This works just like Grid Snapping does in the 3D Viewport. This first button turns snapping on and off, and the second button sets the Snap Size.

Figure 8.5.2 – Use these buttons to set Grid Snapping

To the right of that is the *Zoom to Fit* button. This will center the layout on the screen and zoom in to it. It will zoom in until the layout fills the screen or reaches a 1:1 aspect ratio, whichever comes first.

Figure 8.5.3 – The Zoom to Fit button

The dropdown to the right of that button can be used to see how the layout will look on different devices and screen sizes. There are options for various phones, tablets, laptops, monitors, and HDTVs. The resolution and aspect ratio of the screen size you choose can be seen in the bottom-left corner of the Visual Designer.

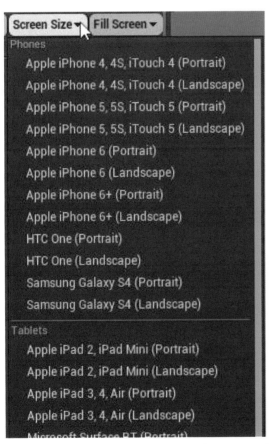

Figure 8.5.4 – You can preview how your layout will look on various screen sizes

The dropdown to the right of that can be used to choose the overall size of the layout relative to the screen size. With this set to *Fill Screen*, the layout will always be the size of the screen it's on. With this set to *Custom*, you can choose a specific size for the layout to be, regardless of the screen it's on. *Custom on Screen* is the same as Custom except there is an additional outline for the screen size itself. *Desired* will cause the bounds of the layout to be just large enough to fit all of the widgets within it while still honoring the spacing set by the Anchors. With *Desired on Screen* you can also see the edges of the screen.

Figure 8.5.5 – Use this menu to adjust the size of the layout relative to the screen size

8.6 Text Widget

The *Text Widget* can be found in the Common category of the Palette. When you first create a Text Widget, it will start out with the default text "Text Block." To change this text, go over to the Details window and edit the *Text* property in the Content category.

Figure 8.6.1 – The Content category of the Text Widget

As you saw earlier, you can set the color of the text and how transparent it is by using the Color & Opacity property. If you check Inherit, it will inherit the settings from the Foreground Color of its next highest parent.

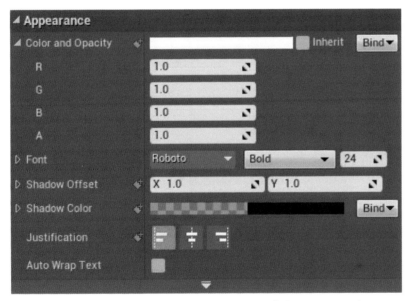

Figure 8.6.2 - The Appearance category of the Text Widget

The *Font* property is where you can set the Font Type, Font Style, and Font Size. Unreal Engine only comes with one font built-in, *Roboto*, so if you want to use different fonts, you will need to import them in yourself. An easy way to do this is to simply go into the

Fonts folder of your operating system and drag-and-drop the fonts you want into the Content Browser. On Windows, you can get to that folder by going to Control Panel > Appearance and Personalization > Fonts.

The next two properties, Shadow Offset and Shadow Color, enable you to add a shadow to your text. By default, the color of *Shadow Color* is set to black, but its opacity is set to be fully transparent, meaning it will be invisible by default. To use the shadow, you will need to increase the Alpha channel so that it will be visible. A value of 1 will make the shadow fully opaque, meaning it cannot be seen through at all.

Figure 8.6.3 – A shadow effect has been added to this text

The *Shadow Offset* property is used to set how far in the X and Y directions the shadow should be located, relative to the base text. If you increase in the X direction, the shadow will move out to the right. At first, this has the effect of making the shadow thicker, but if you keep going, eventually the shadow will completely separate from the base text.

The *Justification* property will simply align the text to the left, center, or right, relative to its container.

Last, is the *Auto Wrap Text* property. With this unchecked, if the text runs out of room in its container, it will simply get cut off. With this checked, once the text reaches the edge of the container, the rest of it will automatically wrap down to the next line.

8.7 Button Widget

The *Button Widget* can be found in the Common category of the Palette. In the Details window, there is an *Appearance* category where you can modify how the button looks.

Figure 8.7.1 – The Appearance category of a Button Widget

Starting with the two color properties, *Color and Opacity* will set the color of the button's content, while *Background Color* will set the color of the button itself. If you were to add a Text Widget as a child of the Button Widget, and then set the Color and Opacity of the button to red, the text will turn red. If you were to set the Background Color to red, the button itself will turn red.

The *Style* property is actually a collection of properties, which in turn have their own sub-properties. The first four properties, *Normal*, *Hovered*, *Pressed*, and *Disabled* each represent a different state of the button. By expanding their menus, you will find several properties you can edit to alter that state's appearance.

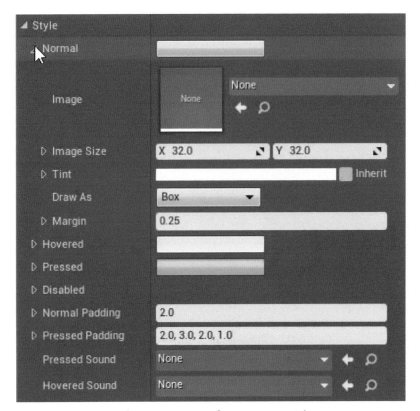

Figure 8.7.2 – Style properties of a Button Widget

For example, if you expanded the Hovered property, and set its *Tint* to purple, then when the mouse cursor hovers over the button, its color will change to purple. Note that if you have set a Background Color, that the Tint will combine with that color. So if the Background Color is blue, and the Tint of the Normal state is yellow, then the button will appear green when in its Normal state.

You can also use an image for the button's background by using the dropdown next to the *Image* property. If you have any colors applied to the button's background, it will use that color as a filter on top of your image.

The next property, *Image Size*, doesn't affect the button when it's in a Canvas Panel. In other Panels, the Image Size property will change the size of the button, regardless of whether or not it actually contains an image.

The *Draw As* property affects how the image is drawn onto the button. With this set to *Image*, it will stretch or shrink the image evenly across the entire button. You also have the option to tile the image horizontally, vertically, or in both directions.

If Draw As is set to *Box*, it will use a more complex set of rules to stretch or shrink the image. With all the margins set to 0, it will appear the same as if it were set to Image. But if the Left Margin increases, it will start taking the left-most portion of the image and shrink it into a thin margin on the left, while stretching out the remaining portion of the image on the right. As the size of the margin increases, more and more of the image goes into the margin, until, finally, all that remains on the right is a tiny sliver of the image which gets stretched across that entire space.

If Draw As is set to *Border*, it will use the image to create a border along the edges of the button, leaving empty space in the middle. You can use the *Margin* property to set the thickness of the border on each edge.

Figure 8.7.3 – The Draw As property of this Button Widget has been set to Border

Next, are a couple of properties used to set the padding for the button's contents. You can set different paddings for when the button is in its Normal state and for when it is Pressed. By default, the Pressed padding has a little more padding on top and a little less on the bottom, which causes the contents of the button to shift down when the button is pressed. This creates the appearance of the button actually being pressed as if it were a 3D object.

You also have the option of having a sound play whenever the button is pressed or hovered over, by using the dropdowns of the *Pressed Sound* and *Hovered Sound* properties, and selecting a sound Asset.

At the very bottom of the Details window, the Button Widget has an *Events* category. Not all widgets have Events tied to them, but those that do will have an Events category.

Figure 8.7.4 – The Events category of a Button Widget

The Button Widget has three events, OnClicked, OnPressed, and OnReleased. The *OnPressed* event fires when the button is pressed. The *OnClicked* and *OnReleased* events will fire once the button has been pressed and then released. By clicking on the green buttons next to their names, you can add a Node for that Event to the graph of this widget. Note that these Events work the same whether you are using the mouse or the keyboard to press the button. So the "click" of the OnClicked Event refers to the Button Widget being clicked, not the clicking of a mouse.

8.8 Border Widget & Image Widget

The *Border Widget* has two main categories, Content and Appearance.

In the *Appearance* category, you can alter the appearance of the border by giving it an image, or by setting its color. So if you wanted a simple black border, you would set the *Brush Color* to black.

Figure 8.8.1 – The Appearance category of a Border Widget

At first glance, the Border Widget will look more like a box than a border. But when you add a child to it, the child will be centered within it, covering up the majority of it, and whatever peeks out around the edges essentially acts as a border.

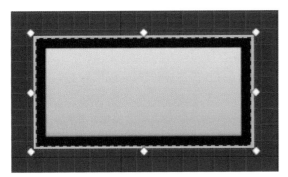

Figure 8.8.2 – A Button Widget inside of a Border Widget

In the *Content* category, you can adjust the padding that is placed around the child of the widget. However thick the padding is, is how thick your border will appear. You can also use this category to adjust the horizontal and vertical alignment of the widget's child, or to set the child's Color and Opacity.

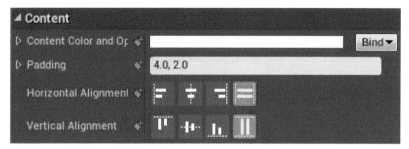

Figure 8.8.3 – The Content category of a Border Widget

The only difference between the Border Widget and the *Image Widget* is that the Border Widget has a Content category since it is especially designed to have children, and the Image Widget is not.

8.9 Progress Bar Widget

The *Progress Bar Widget* is often used to display things like the amount of health, magic, or energy a player has remaining. It will measure these values by percentage by using the *Percent* property of the *Progress* category.

Figure 8.9.1 – The Progress category of the Progress Bar Widget

With Percent at 0, the bar will be completely empty. If it was set to 0.5, the bar would be 50% filled, and if it was set to the max value of 1.0, the bar would be 100% filled. The Percent property is normally bound to the variable it is meant to represent so that it will automatically update as that variable's value changes.

Figure 8.9.2 – A Progress Bar Widget with its Percent set to 0.5

The color that is used to fill the bar can be set with the *Fill Color and Opacity* property.

Figure 8.9.3 – The Appearance category of the Progress Bar Widget

You also have the option of using an image to fill the Progress Bar or have an image used as its background. In the *Style* category, the *Fill Image* property is used for the image that will fill the bar, and the *Background Image* property will specify the image that will be used for its background. If you still want the background to be a solid color, just not grey, you can leave the Image property blank, but choose a color for the *Tint* property of the Background Image, and it will set the background to that color.

Figure 8.9.4 – The Style category of the Progress Bar Widget

The default direction that the bar will fill is from left to right, but you have the option of having it fill in different directions, such as right to left or top to bottom, by setting the *Bar Fill Type* property.

If the *Is Marquee* property is checked, the Progress Bar will change from a genuine Progress Bar into a *Marquee*.

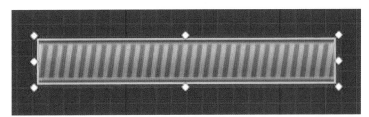

Figure 8.9.5 – A Progress Bar Widget with its Is Marquee property set to True

A Marquee is a bar that, instead of filling up, shows continual movement. This is generally used to indicate to the user that some action is taking place, when it is unknown how long it will take to complete, and thus can't be represented by a regular Progress Bar. An example of a Marquee would be when a program crashes in Windows and it gives you the "Windows is checking for a solution" message. That green bar is a Marquee.

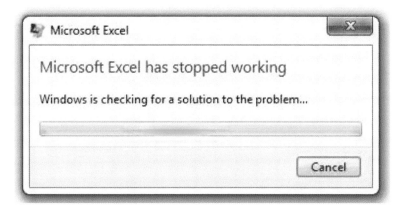

Figure 8.9.6 – This bar with the green in it is an example of a Marquee

In the Style category, you can set an image to use for the Marquee with the *Marquee Image* property. If you change the X value of the Image Size property of the Marquee Image, it will increase or decrease the speed of the Marquee.

8.10 Check Box Widget

The *Check Box Widget* gives you the ability to add checkboxes to your interface.

Check Box Properties

The Check Box Widget's initial state can be set by the *Checked State* property of the Appearance category. This can be set to *Unchecked*, *Checked*, or *Undetermined*. The Undetermined setting can be used to determine whether or not the user actually interacted with the Check Box.

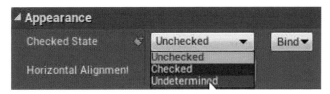

Figure 8.10.1 – The Appearance category of the Check Box Widget

In the Style category, the first property is *Check Box Type*. This can be set to either *Check Box* or *Toggle Button*. According to Epic Games, you use the Check Box setting for a traditional checkbox while you use the Toggle Button when you want to provide your own image. However, you can use your own image for the checkbox regardless of which setting Check Box Type is set to, so this blurs this distinction quite a bit.

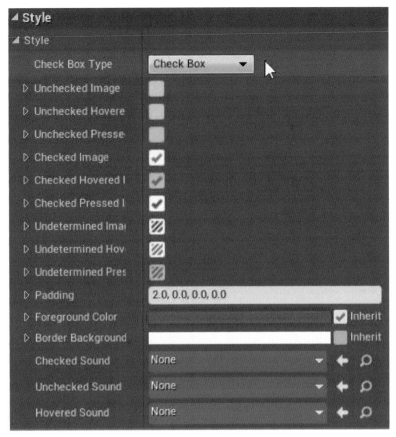

Figure 8.10.2 – The Style category of the Check Box Widget

For practical purposes, the only real difference between the two settings is that the traditional Check Box is useful for labeling. If you add a Text Widget as a child of the Check Box when its type is set to Check Box, it will automatically align the Text Widget to the right. But with the Check Box set to Toggle Button, child widgets will not align.

With Check Box Type set to Check Box, you use the Foreground Color property to set its color, or to add a tint to a supplied image. With it set to Toggle Button, you use the Border Background property to set the color or tint.

Also in the Style category, you can change the appearance of the Check Box for all the different combinations of possible states. So all the different combinations of Unchecked, Checked, and Undetermined, and Normal, Hovered, and Pressed. You can use an image instead of the default appearance, and whether you use an image or not, you can change the size of the checkbox using the Image Size property.

The *Padding* property is used to add padding around the children of the Check Box. For example, if you add a Text Widget to the Check Box and then increase the Left Padding of the Check Box, it will add padding to the left of the Text Widget which will push it further to the right.

There are also some properties to have the Check Box play a sound when it is checked, unchecked, or hovered over.

Checking the State of the Check Box

When you want to see what state the Check Box is currently in, there are a few ways to do this. One way is to make the Check Box a variable and get the information from that variable. At the top of the Details window, if the *Is Variable* checkbox is checked, it will store the Check Box Widget in a variable. The textbox to the left is used to name the variable.

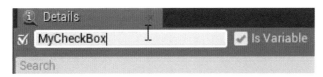

Figure 8.10.3 – You can store widgets in a variable by checking the Is Variable property at the top of the Details window

This variable will be created automatically and will be available in the Graph tab. If you add the variable to the graph, there are a couple of Function Nodes that you can connect it to, to get information about the state of the Check Box Widget.

The first Node is called *Is Checked*. This will output a Boolean value of True if the Check Box is Checked, and a value of False if the state of the Check Box is either Unchecked or Undetermined. So you wouldn't want to use this function if you plan on using Undetermined states.

Figure 8.10.4 – The Is Checked Node

If you do plan on using Undetermined states, you will want to use the *Get Checked State Node* instead. This will return a variable of type *ECheckBoxState Enum*. Enum variables were not covered in the Variables section, so they will be covered now. An *Enum*, which is short for "Enumerated Value" is a type of variable that can only hold a value from a finite set of predefined options. For example, there could be a Weekday Enum that can only store one of seven possible values - Sunday, Monday, Tuesday, etc. The ECheckBoxState Enum can only have a value of either Checked, Unchecked, or Undetermined.

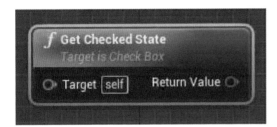

Figure 8.10.5 – The Get Checked State Node

You will generally use Enums in conjunction with Switch statements, which were covered in the section on flow control. So you will want to drag out a wire from the Return Value pin of the Get Checked State Node, and add a *Switch on ECheckBoxState Node*. From there, execution will flow through one of the three output pins, Unchecked, Checked, or Undetermined, based on which state the Check Box is in.

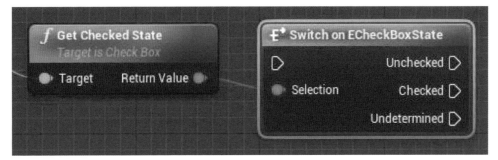

Figure 8.10.6 – Execution will flow through one of three pins on the Switch on ECheckBoxState Node based on the state of the Check Box Widget that has been passed into the Get Checked State function

Another way to get the state of a Check Box is to bind it to a variable and get the information directly from that variable. So you can create either a Boolean variable or an ECheckBoxState Enum variable and then bind that to the Checked State property. This saves you the step of having to call the Is Checked or Get Checked State functions. You will have a variable that will automatically be updated with the latest state of the Check Box.

Finally, if something might need to occur immediately when the state of the Check Box is changed, you will want to use the *OnCheckStateChanged Event*. This Event will fire every time the Check Box is checked or unchecked, and it includes a Boolean return value which will tell you which of those states it was just changed to.

Figure 8.10.7 – The OnCheckStateChanged Event Node

8.11 Horizontal Box & Vertical Box

So far, the only Panel that has been covered is the Canvas Panel, which allows for absolute layout. This is good when you want a high level of manual control over the placement of widgets, but it's not the best for aligning widgets.

There are several other Panels which are much more useful for aligning widgets, and one of those is the *Horizontal Box*. The Horizontal Box is comprised of a single row of slots of equal height. It's useful for aligning widgets side-by-side.

For example, if you placed three Button Widgets into a Horizontal Box, they would stack up side-by-side. If you wanted to change their order, you could select one of them and use the arrows that appear to move them to the slot to the left or right. If you wanted to move all of them, you could move them all as a group by moving the Horizontal Box itself, and they would all remain aligned with each other.

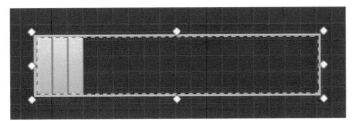

Figure 8.11.1 – Three Button Widgets in a Horizontal Box Panel

If you selected one of the buttons, you would see that the properties in its Slot category are different than what we've been seeing because the button is in a *Horizontal Box Slot* as opposed to a Canvas Panel Slot.

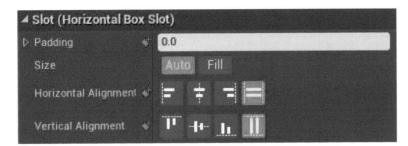

Figure 8.11.2 – Properties of the Horizontal Box Slot

The *Padding* property can be used to add padding around the content of the slot.

By default, the *Size* property will be set to *Auto*. With it set to Auto, the slot will be just big enough to fit its contents. So if the width of a button inside the slot was increased, the slot would automatically widen to fit it. If Size is set to *Fill*, the slot will expand to take up the rest of the room available.

Figure 8.11.3 – The Size property of the third button has been set to Fill

If other slots are set to Fill, the amount of space that each slot uses relative to each other is determined by the value to the right of the Fill button. This value can be any number between 0 and 1. For example, if there were three slots, and the first was set to 1.0 and the remaining two were set to 0.5, the first slot would be twice the size of the other two.

The next two properties determine how the content is aligned within the slot. By default, these are set to Fill. So note that the Fill settings of the Alignment properties refer to the content of the slot filling up the slot, while the Fill setting of the Size property refers to the slot filling up the Horizontal Box.

The *Vertical Box* works just like the Horizontal Box, except the widgets placed in it will stack vertically instead.

Figure 8.11.4 – Two Button Widgets in a Vertical Box Panel

8.12 Grid Panel & Uniform Grid Panel

Uniform Grid Panel

The *Uniform Grid Panel* can have both rows and columns of slots and what makes it special is that all of its slots will always be the same size as each other.

By default, children added to a Uniform Grid Panel will be placed in Row 0, Column 0, which will always be the upper-leftmost slot of the Panel. If you want to place a child in a different row or column, you can move it using the arrow buttons, or use the Row and Column properties in the Slot category. Also, by default, content will be aligned to the left and top of the slot.

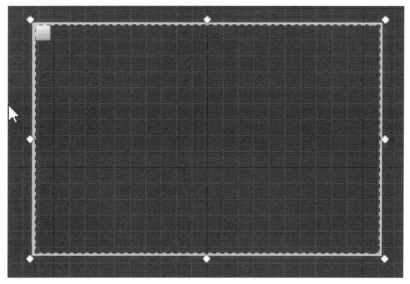

Figure 8.12.1 – A Button Widget located in row 0, column 0 of a Uniform Grid Panel

The Uniform Grid Panel has three unique properties within a category called *Child Layout*. The first is *Slot Padding*, which will simply apply the same amount of padding to each of the slots.

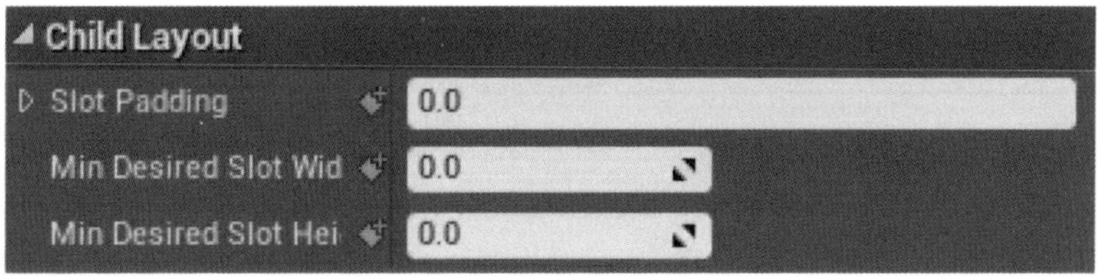

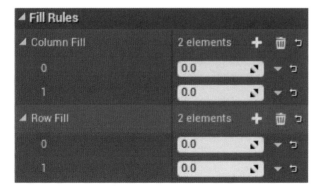

Figure 8.12.2 – The Child Layout category of a Uniform Grid Panel

The next two properties, the *Minimum Desired Slot Width* and *Minimum Desired Slot Height*, apply when the Panel's *Size to Content* property is checked. With Size to Property unchecked, the content is sized to match the size of the slots. But with Size to Content checked, the slots will resize to match the sizes of the content. The "Minimum Desired" properties, however, can override the Size to Content property, if the content doesn't force the slot to be at least the minimum size specified.

Grid Panel

The *Grid Panel* is similar to the Uniform Grid Panel, but its slots can be different sizes from each other.

The easiest way to use a Grid Panel is to first specify the number of rows and columns it will have and then add the content. To add rows and columns, use the *Fill Rules* category. For example, to make a 2x2 grid, click the add button of the *Column Fill* property twice and click the add button of the *Row Fill* property twice.

Figure 8.12.3 – The Fill Rules category of a Grid Panel with two rows and two columns

You can specify the amount of the space each row or column should occupy relative to each other by using the textboxes to the right. These work just like the Horizontal or Vertical Box did, with the exception that these values can be set to any number, not just those between 0 and 1.

Grid Slot Properties

The first two properties of a Grid Slot are *Horizontal Alignment* and *Vertical Alignment*. These are used to change the alignment of the content within the slot. By default, they are set to Fill.

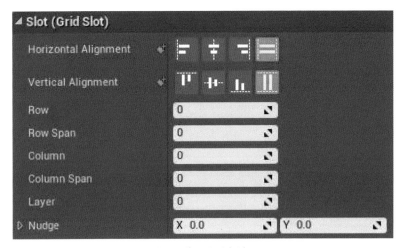

Figure 8.12.4 – Properties of a Grid Slot

In addition to using the arrows to position content, you can directly set the row and column it should be placed in by setting the *Row* and/or *Column* property. Just like the Uniform Grid Panel, the Grid Panel is zero-based, so 0 is the first row, and 1 is the second row and so on.

Unlike the Uniform Grid Panel, the slots of the Grid Panel have the ability to span rows and columns. For these span properties, *Row Span* and *Column Span*, the values 0 and 1 do the same thing, which is to have the slot maintain its default behavior of only occupying a single row and column. But if the Row Span of a slot were changed to 2, it would span 2 rows. Or if Column Span was changed to 2, it would span two columns.

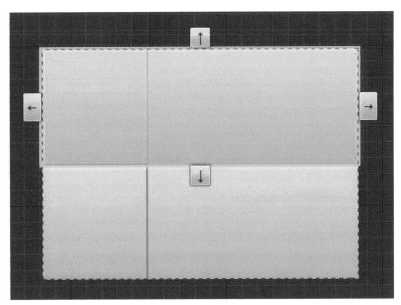

Figure 8.12.5 – A Button Widget in row 0, column 0 with a Column Span of 2

The next property, *Layer*, comes into play when widgets overlap. This property is just like the ZOrder property of the Canvas Panel Slot. Widgets in slots with higher Layer numbers will be drawn last, and thus drawn on top of other widgets in slots with lower numbers. Also, if a user clicks in the overlapping area, the widget in the slot with the highest number will register the click.

The final property, *Nudge*, is used to add an offset to the location of the slot. So if you wanted to move a slot to the right 20 units, you would enter "20" for the X value. Note that you need to compile the Blueprint in order for changes to the Nudge property to be reflected in the Visual Designer.

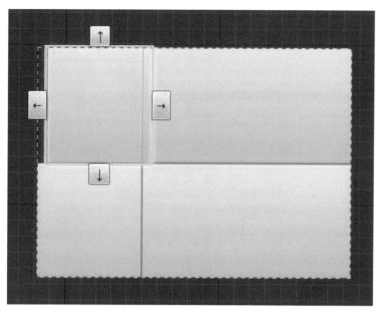

Figure 8.12.6 – A Button Widget that has been nudged 20 units to the right

8.13 Chapter 8 Quiz

1. What does HUD stand for?

2. What visual-based framework does Unreal Engine 4 use for developing user interfaces?

3. What type of Blueprint is used to create user interfaces in Unreal Engine 4?

4. What Node takes a widget as input and then displays that widget on the screen?

5. True or False: Whatever color you set the Color and Opacity to in the Root Widget will be applied to all child widgets and will be combined with the color of the child itself.

6. What type of Panel is best for absolute positioning of its children?

7. What type of Panel is best for perfectly aligning its children evenly with one another?

8. What is the ZOrder property used for?

9. What does it mean when a widget's Visibility property is set to Hidden?

10. How would you use a Progress Bar Widget to automatically represent the value of a numerical variable during runtime?

11. What is an Enum variable?

Answers

1. Heads Up Display

2. Unreal Motion Graphics (UMG)

3. Widget Blueprint

4. Add To Viewport Node

5. True

6. Canvas Panel

7. Uniform Grid Panel

8. Used to determine the order in which widgets get drawn to the screen and, thus, for widgets in the same location, determines which widget overlaps which.

9. The widget will be invisible to the user, and cannot be interacted with by the user, but it will take up space in the layout.

10. Bind that variable to the Progress Bar's Percent property.

11. A type of variable that can only hold a value from a finite set of predefined options.

9

Audio

9.1 Audio Overview & Sound Waves

This chapter will cover the use of audio within the Unreal Engine, so that you will be able to add dialogue, music, and sound effects to your game. The Audio folder in the Starter Content contains some existing audio Assets you can use as you read this chapter.

Unreal Engine uses *.wav* files, pronounced "wave," to handle audio. If you have some audio you want to use that's in a different format, such as an MP3, you will first need to convert it to a wave file, which will be covered later in the chapter.

When you import a wave file into Unreal Engine, it will become a *Sound Wave* Asset in the Content Browser, and its icon will have a black background with the actual waveform of that sound shown in white. If the wave has more than one channel, there will be a separate waveform for each channel.

Figure 9.1.1 – A Sound Wave

If you want to combine sounds and/or add effects to them, you can do so using a *Sound Cue*, which is represented by an icon with a blue background and a picture of a speaker and waveform. Note that, unlike the Sound Wave, the waveform on the Sound Cue icon is generic and doesn't represent the actual waveform that is produced by the Asset.

Figure 9.1.2 – A Sound Cue

Ambient Sound Actor

If you drag either a Sound Wave or a Sound Cue into your Level, it will create what's called an *Ambient Sound Actor*.

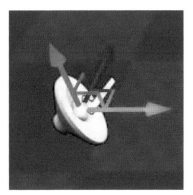

Figure 9.1.3 – An Ambient Sound Actor

It will automatically assign whatever Asset you dragged in, as the Asset for that Actor's *Sound* property.

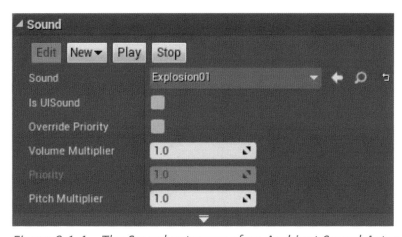

Figure 9.1.4 – The Sound category of an Ambient Sound Actor

If you want to preview the sound, you can use the Play and Stop buttons, located above the Sound property. For Sound Cues, you can use the Edit button to open the Sound Cue in the *Sound Cue Editor*. If you want to create a new Sound Cue to use for the Actor, you can use the New button.

By default, any sounds coming from an Ambient Sound Actor will be paused when the game is paused. If you want a sound to be able to play while the game is paused, you would need to set the *Is UISound* property to True.

You also have the option of adjusting the Ambient Sound Actor's *Volume* or *Pitch*.

The *Priority* and *Override Priority* properties are used when the Actor is playing multiple instances of its sound concurrently. The concept of concurrency will be covered later in the section.

By default, an Ambient Sound Actor's *Auto Activate* property is set to True. With it set to True, the sound will play as soon as the Actor is created. By default, the Ambient Sound Actor will only play its sound once. If you want the sound to be continuous, you will need to set it to loop. With a Sound Wave, this can be accomplished by setting its *Looping* property to True. With a Sound Cue, this is done by using a *Looping Node*.

Sound Wave Properties

If you want to edit the properties of a Sound Wave, you simply need to double-click on it in the Content Browser.

You can set the compression of the wave using the *Compression Quality* property. This can have a value from 1 to 100, where lower numbers represent more compression and higher numbers represent better quality. So if you want the sound to sound as good as it can, and you're not worried about the file size, you would want to set this to a high number. If you don't care about the quality of the sound and you just need to save space somewhere, you could set this to a low number.

Figure 9.1.5 – The Compression category of a Sound Wave

In the *Subtitles* category, you can add subtitles to the Sound Wave, and edit their properties. To add a subtitle, go to the *Subtitles* property and click the plus sign. Then you enter the text of the subtitle in the *Text* property and the time it should appear on the screen in the *Time* property. The Time property refers to the amount of time that has elapsed since the Sound Wave began playing.

Figure 9.1.6 – The Subtitles category of a Sound Wave

There is also a *Spoken Text* property. The difference between the Spoken Text property and the Text property is that the Text property is for the text that should appear on the screen, while the Spoken Text property is for the dialogue that was actually spoken. For example, there might be the word "angrily" in brackets indicating that the speaker is speaking in an angry tone. Or if the subtitles are in a different language, then obviously the two texts will be different.

The *Mature* property is used to flag a piece of audio that contains mature content, such as adult language. This can be used to more easily create a "clean" version of your game later, by having the ability to filter out all mature content.

By default, the Engine will automatically wrap your subtitles to the next line if they get too long, but if you don't want the Engine to do this - for example, if you have already split the subtitles manually - you can set *Manual Word Wrap* to True to disable automatic wrapping. If you want to force all subtitles to only display on one line, you can set the *Single Line* property to True.

The final Subtitle property is *Comment*. If you plan on having your game translated into other languages, the Comment property can be useful for adding contextual information about the piece of dialogue that the translator can use to create a more accurate translation.

In the *Sound* category, you can adjust the volume and pitch of the Sound Wave, and you can also place it into a *Sound Group*. So you can specify if it should go in Effects, UI, Music, or Voice. Or, if it doesn't fit into any of those categories, you can just leave it in the Default group. Groups are useful for being able to apply a setting to an entire group of related Sound Waves, instead of having to apply that setting to each individual one.

Figure 9.1.7 – The Sound category of a Sound Wave

Sound Class is similar in concept to Sound Group, except it's more robust, you can save and reuse Sound Classes, and you can create your own custom groupings.

Below that are some read-only properties that provide some important information about the Sound Wave, including the number of channels it has, its sample rate, how long it is, and the file path to the actual wave file that the Sound Wave Asset uses.

Figure 9.1.8 – The Info and Import Settings categories of a Sound Wave are read-only

The *Concurrency* category is used to specify what should happen when multiple instances of the Sound Wave are played at the same time. If you want to use pre-existing Concurrency Settings, you will need to set the Override Concurrency property to False, and then select the settings using the dropdown. If you want to specify new concurrency settings, then you need to set Override Concurrency to True, and then you will be able to expand the Concurrency Overrides property.

Figure 9.1.9 – The Concurrency category of a Sound Wave

The *Max Count* property specifies how many instances of the sound are allowed to be playing at once. The *Limit to Owner* property specifies if the Max Count should only be applied per sound Actor, or if it should be applied to all instances of the Sound Wave that are being played from any sound Actor.

If the Max Count is reached and another instance of the sound tries to play, you can set how the conflict should be resolved using the *Resolution Rule* property. For example, you could set it to prevent the new instance from being played, or set it so that the oldest instance is stopped to make room for the new instance, and so on.

With the *Volume Scale* property, you can cause older instances to become quieter as new instances of this sound are played. With this set to 1.0, there will be no difference in volume. But if you set this below 1.0, older instances will become quieter and quieter as newer instances are played, and the lower the number is, the more dramatic the effect.

This *Priority* property, along with the Priority property we saw earlier on the Ambient Sound Actor, is used in conjunction with setting the Resolution Rule to *Stop Lowest Priority*.

Below the Concurrency category is the *Attenuation* category. The concept of attenuation will be covered in detail later in the chapter.

Play Sound Nodes

We already saw how to have a sound play immediately when the Level begins, but often times, you won't want a sound to be played until certain conditions are met, or a certain event is triggered. In these cases, you can use Blueprints to specify when the sound should be played.

If you go into the Level Blueprint, open the Node Menu, and type "Play Sound," you will see several Nodes available for playing a sound. For one thing, you can choose to either play a sound, or spawn a sound. The difference is that when you spawn a sound you have control over it. You can choose to stop playing the sound at any point, or modify its properties. But when you play a sound, you don't have any control over it. You can't modify it or stop it. It will continue playing until it's finished, and if it's set to loop it will continue playing for the rest of the game.

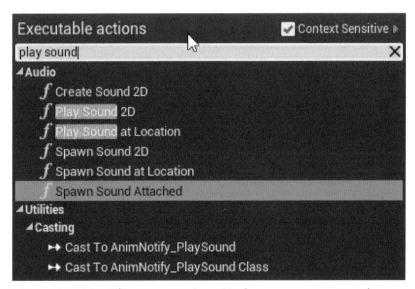

Figure 9.1.10 – There are various Nodes you can use to play a sound

You can also choose to have a sound come from a certain location in the game, or make it a 2D sound which will be heard at the same volume regardless of your location in the game. If you use one of the location Nodes, such as *Play Sound at Location*, you will need to pass in the location where you want the sound to play from. If you wanted it to play from the location of a certain Actor, you could use the *GetActorLocation* Node to get that Actor's location. Or, with the *Spawn Sound Attached Node*, you can attach a sound to an Actor directly and the sound will travel with that Actor.

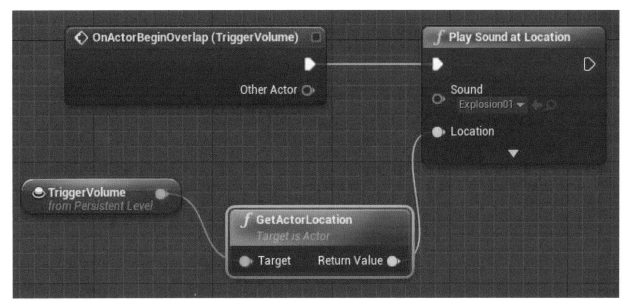

Figure 9.1.11 – This logic will play a sound, emanating from the location of a Trigger Volume, whenever any Actor enters the Trigger Volume

9.2 Sound Cues

Sound Cues use existing Sound Waves to create new sounds, by combining Sound Waves and/or adjusting their properties or adding effects to them. To create a new Sound Cue, click the Add New button in the Content Browser, scroll down to Sounds, select Sound Cue, and then give it a name.

To edit a Sound Cue, simply double-click on it to open it in the Sound Cue Editor. The Sound Cue Editor uses a node-based graph very similar to Blueprints. However, it uses its own specialized Nodes instead of the types of Nodes that are available in Blueprints.

The basic idea is that you start with one or more Nodes on the left that represent Sound Waves, and then you connect those Sound Waves to Nodes in the middle that will combine and modify them. Finally, whatever gets outputted to the *Output Node* on the right is the sound that the Sound Cue will actually play.

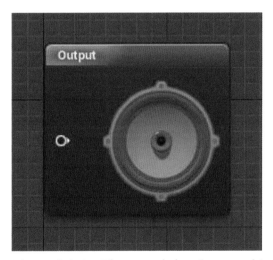

Figure 9.2.1 – The sound that is passed into the Output Node is the sound that the Sound Cue will play

To hear what the output will sound like, click the *Play Cue* button in the Toolbar. To hear what an individual Node sounds like by itself, select that Node and click the *Play Node* button.

Figure 9.2.2 – The Play Cue and Play Node buttons

You can add Nodes like you do in Blueprints, by right-clicking in the graph and selecting from a Node Menu. Or you can drag-and-drop Nodes from the Palette Window on the right side of the Editor.

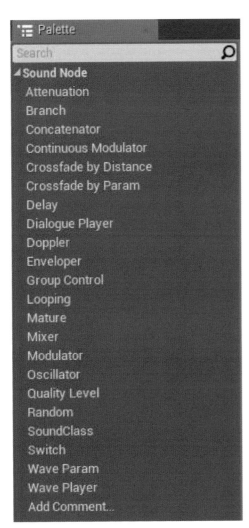

Figure 9.2.3 – The Palette Window in the Sound Cue Editor contains several Nodes you can use to modify sounds

Audio Nodes

A *Wave Player Node* is used to output Sound Waves. If you select it, you can edit its properties in the Details Panel on the left. The *Sound Wave* property will specify which Sound Wave the Node should output.

Figure 9.2.4 – The Wave Player Node

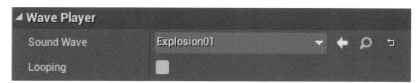

Figure 9.2.5 – Properties of the Wave Player Node

A *Looping Node* will take a sound as input, and output that sound as a loop. In the Details Panel, you can choose to have it loop a specific amount of times, or have it loop continuously.

Figure 9.2.6 – The Looping Node

Figure 9.2.7 – Properties of the Looping Node

The *Delay Node* can be used to add a delay before a sound is played. Each time the Delay Node is activated, the amount of delay will be a random value between the *Delay Min* and *Delay Max*. So if you set this to 1 and 3, for example, each time the sound is played, the delay will be between 1 and 3 seconds. If you wanted the delay to always be the same value, you would need to enter that value for both the Min and Max properties.

Figure 9.2.8 – The Delay Node

Figure 9.2.9 – Properties of the Delay Node

The *Doppler Node* can be used to add the Doppler effect to a sound. This is the effect that occurs when sounds, such as the siren of an ambulance, increase in pitch as they move towards you and decrease in pitch as they move away. The *Doppler Intensity* property can be used to specify how pronounced this effect should be, with higher values increasing the effect.

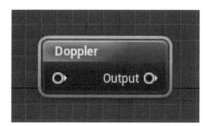

Figure 9.2.10 – The Doppler Node

Figure 9.2.11 – Properties of the Doppler Node

The *Modulator Node* can be used to play a sound at a random pitch and volume each time it's played. This can be used to make the audio sound slightly different each time so as not to get repetitive. The range of the random values generated can be set in the Details Panel.

Figure 9.2.12 – The Modulator Node

Figure 9.2.13 – Properties of the Modulator Node

The *Oscillator Node* can be used to add a continuous modulation of volume and pitch within a single instance of a sound being played. The first two properties are used to enable the modulation of the volume and/or pitch. *Amplitude* refers to the height of the Sound Wave, with larger waves producing louder volumes. *Frequency* affects the pitch of a sound, with higher frequencies resulting in higher pitches. The remaining properties deal with more advanced wave physics, with the *Offset* properties controlling the wave's phase and the *Center* properties controlling the center of oscillation.

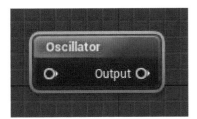

Figure 9.2.14 – The Oscillator Node

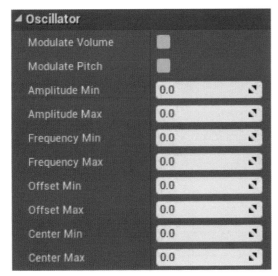

Figure 9.2.15 – Properties of the Oscillator Node

In addition to Nodes that alter sounds, the Palette also contains many useful Nodes for combining sounds. A *Mixer Node* takes two or more sounds as input and outputs all of those sounds being played simultaneously. In the Details Panel, you can adjust the volumes of each input.

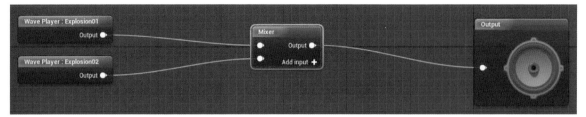

Figure 9.2.16 – The Mixer Node in use – this logic combines two different sounds and plays them simultaneously

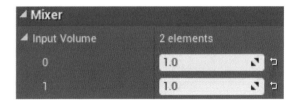

Figure 9.2.17 – Properties of the Mixer Node

The *Concatenator Node* is just like the Mixer Node, except that instead of playing its input sounds simultaneously, it plays them one after the other.

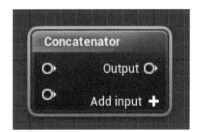

Figure 9.2.18 – The Concatenator Node

A *Random Node* will randomly output just one of its input sounds each time it's activated. By default, each sound has an equal chance of being played each time, but you can change this using the *Weights* property. For example, if you set the weight of the first sound to 2, and leave the weight of the second sound at 1, then the first sound has twice the chance of being played each time.

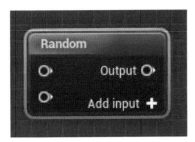

Figure 9.2.19 – The Random Node

You can use the *Preselect at Level Load* property to trim down the number of possible inputs that can be selected from. For example, if the Random Node has 10 inputs and Preselect at Level Load is set to 5, then as soon as the Level loaded, it would randomly select five of the inputs, and then only randomly select from those five each time the Sound Cue was played. This can be used to trim down memory usage for Random Nodes that have several inputs. Note that this Node doesn't have any effect when simulating your game, it will only work when playing a build outside of the Editor.

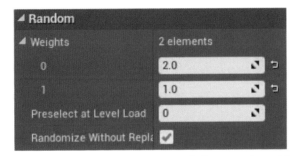

Figure 9.2.20 – Properties of the Random Node

With the *Randomize Without Replacement* property checked, it will ensure that each sound gets played once before the same sound can be randomly selected again.

The *Branch Node* will output one of its input sounds based on the value of a Boolean variable. In the Details Panel, you use the *Bool Parameter Name* property to specify the name of the Boolean variable that should be evaluated. If that Boolean has a value of True, whatever sound is connected to the *True* pin will be outputted. If the value is False, the sound connected to the *False* pin will be outputted, and if the Boolean has a value of Null, then the sound connected to the *Parameter Unset* pin will be used.

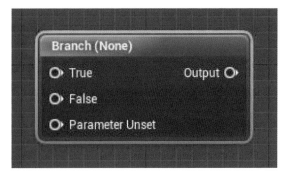

Figure 9.2.21 – The Branch Node

Figure 9.2.22 – Properties of the Branch Node

The *Switch Node* is just like the Branch Node, except it outputs a sound based on the value of an Integer variable instead of a Boolean variable.

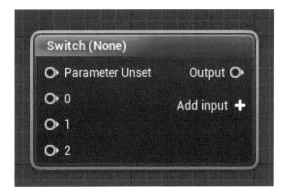

Figure 9.2.23 – The Switch Node

9.3 Attenuation

Attenuation is a scientific term that refers to the reduction in strength of a signal. In the case of an audio signal, this refers to the decrease in volume that occurs due to distance. In Unreal Engine, you have the ability to edit the attenuation properties of the sounds in your game, affecting the rate at which their volumes decrease across distances.

When it's selected, the Ambient Sound Actor will have two spheres around it, an inner sphere and an outer sphere. At any point within the inner sphere, the sound will be heard at 100% volume. Going from the outer edge of the inner sphere, to the outer edge of the outer sphere, the volume will decrease from 100% to zero.

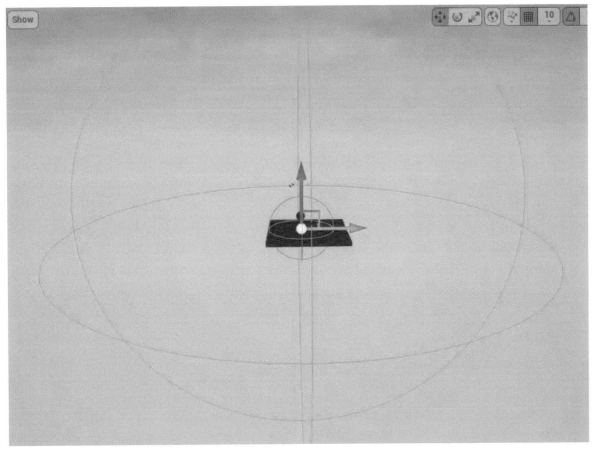

Figure 9.3.1 – The inner and outer attenuation spheres of an Ambient Sound Actor

In the Details Panel, under the *Attenuation* category, you can edit the sizes of these spheres. Note that the *Override Attenuation* property needs to be checked in order to edit the attenuation properties.

Figure 9.3.2 – The Attenuation category of an Ambient Sound Actor

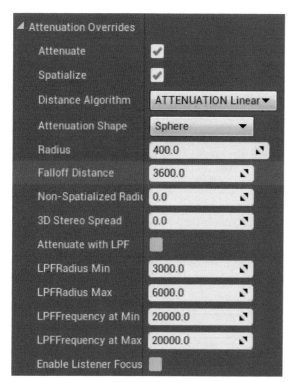

Figure 9.3.3 – If the Override Attenuation property is checked, you can expand the Attenuation Overrides menu

To change the size of the inner sphere, the area in which the sound is heard at full volume, you use the *Radius* property. As you change the size of the inner sphere, the size of the outer sphere changes as well. This is because the outer sphere is defined by the *Falloff Distance*, the distance from the edge of the inner sphere to the edge of the outer sphere, as opposed to being defined by absolute size. When you adjust the Falloff Distance, it will change the size of the outer sphere, making the sound audible at greater distances.

You also have the ability to change the *Attenuation Shape*. By default, spheres are used, as this is the most natural way that sound will attenuate. But if, for example, you had a sound coming from within a rectangular room, you might want to use the Box shape in order to better fit the attenuation to the shape of the room.

Attenuation Curves

As mentioned already, in the area described by the Falloff Distance, the sound will go from 100% volume to zero. But the rate at which this occurs can be adjusted, by setting the *Distance Algorithm* that should be used to define the *Attenuation Curve*. By default, this will use a *Linear curve*, meaning the volume will decrease evenly.

Using the *Logarithmic curve*, the volume will decrease more rapidly at first, then the rate of decrease will slow as the sound approaches the bounds of the attenuation shape. The *LogReverse curve*, as its name indicates, is the reverse of that. The volume will decrease slowly at first, then more rapidly.

The *Inverse curve* is similar to the Logarithmic curve except the volume decreases extremely rapidly at first, then very slowly for the remainder of the distance. The *NaturalSound curve* is somewhere in-between the Logarithmic curve and the Inverse curve, and is supposed to represent the most natural attenuation curve that sounds have in the real world.

Finally, you can create your own custom attenuation curves, using the tool of the *Custom Attenuation Curve* property, which creates curves the same way the Timeline Editor did in the section on Timelines. So you hold down the *Shift* key and left-click in the graph to add a new point on the curve. Then you can click and drag on those points, or manually adjust their locations, to change the shape of the curve.

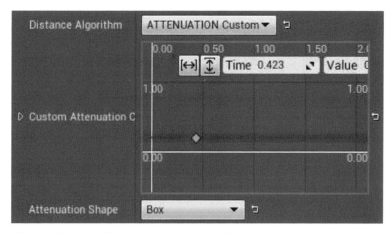

Figure 9.3.4 – Creating a custom attenuation curve

Spatialization

Another property of sound that can be set in the Attenuation category is *Spatialization*. This refers to sound being heard in 3D. For example, in the real world, if a sound is coming from your left, your brain can discern this because the sound will be slightly louder in your left ear than in your right ear. You can mimic this in a game by having sounds coming from the left be louder in the left speaker than in the right speaker. With the *Allow Spatialization* property checked, and the *Spatialize* property itself checked, the sound will exhibit that behavior in the game.

One thing regarding Spatialization, that may seem counterintuitive at first, is that, in order for Spatialization to work, the sound must be *mono*, meaning it only has one channel of output. This is because sounds in *stereo* already have the relative volumes defined for each speaker output. So you need to use mono sounds, so that the Engine can determine the relative volumes itself, based on the rotation of your character relative to the sound.

Attenuation Hierarchy

At the highest level, you can create an Attenuation Asset, that can be saved and applied to multiple sound Assets. To create a new *Sound Attenuation Asset*, click Add New, go to Sounds, then select Sound Attenuation. You can double-click on it to edit its properties, which are the standard set of attenuation properties that were just covered.

You can apply this Sound Attenuation to as many sound objects as you want, and then you only need to make changes for the entire group in one place. For example, if you open a Sound Cue, under the Attenuation Settings property, you can select the Sound Attenuation Asset you created and it will apply those attenuation properties to the Sound Cue.

Figure 9.3.5 – Applying a Sound Attenuation Asset to a Sound Cue

But if you decide you want to set different settings for the Sound Cue, you can check the Override Attenuation property and that will cause the Attenuation Settings property to be ignored, and will instead use the settings defined in the Sound Cue itself.

Now let's say you drag several instances of the Sound Cue into your Level and you want to change the settings for just one of the instances, without changing the settings of the Sound Cue itself. You can select that instance and then edit its Attenuation properties directly in the Details Panel by checking the Override Attenuation property. Or you can choose an existing Sound Attenuation Asset to use just for that instance.

9.4 Importing and Converting Audio

Most of the time, importing audio files into Unreal Engine will be as straightforward as importing any other type of file. You can either click the Import button in the Content Browser and browse to the file you want to import, or you can simply drag and drop the file directly into the Content Browser.

If the file is a wave file, formatted the way Unreal Engine likes it, the file will be converted to a Sound Wave Asset which you can then use as you like. For Unreal Engine to successfully import an audio file, it must be an uncompressed, 16-bit wave file. But if you try to import an audio file that isn't in the right format, such as an MP3, or an 8-bit wave, you will get an error message.

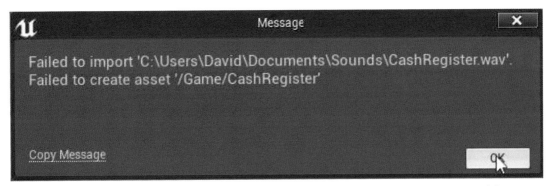

Figure 9.4.1 – Error message when trying to import audio in an unsupported format

Audacity

To get the file into the proper format so that the Engine can import it, you simply need to open the file in an application that can read it, and then export it back out in the proper format. One program that can do this is Audacity. It is free to download and use, can read many different types of audio files in various formats, and it can export those files in a format which the Unreal Engine can read.

The easiest way to find a copy of Audacity to download is to simply go to your favorite search engine and type "download Audacity" and click on the first result. Or you can just type in the following address directly - *audacityteam.org/download*. From there, click on the link that corresponds to your operating system, click on the "installer" link, and then run the .exe file that is downloaded.

If you are running Windows 10, this will probably still work. However, if you get an error message when trying to open a file in Audacity, go back to the first page and click on the link in the line "Windows 10 may require appropriate audio drivers" and then follow the instructions from there.

Once you have Audacity installed, converting your audio files into the proper formatting is pretty simple. First, go to File > Open, and open the file you want converted. If you get a Warning message, simply leave the default choice selected and click "OK." Now, go back up to the File menu and click on "Export Audio." Give the new file a name and make sure the type selected is "WAVE signed 16 bit PCM" which should be the default choice. Now click on "Save," and when the Edit Metadata box pops up, you can simply press OK without making any changes.

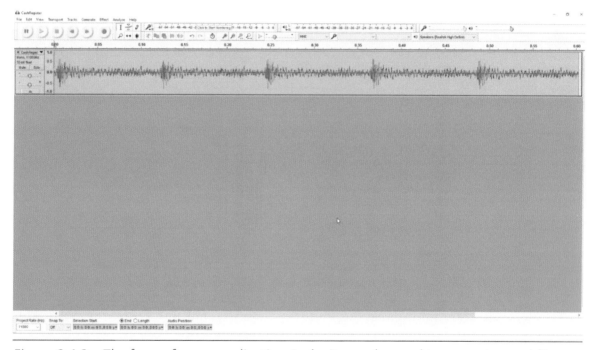

Figure 9.4.2 – The free software application Audacity can be used to convert sound files into a format that Unreal Engine will accept

The file should now be properly formatted, and when you drag-and-drop it into the Content Browser, it should import it into the project without any problems.

9.5 Chapter 9 Quiz

1. What file format does Unreal Engine use for audio files?

2. What type of Asset uses existing Sound Waves to create new sounds, by combining them and/or adjusting their properties or adding effects to them?

3. What type of Actor is used to play Sound Waves or Sound Cues?

4. What would be the result of increasing the value of the Compression Quality property of a Sound Wave?

5. What is the difference between playing a sound and spawning a sound?

6. What effect occurs when sounds, such as the siren of an ambulance, increase in pitch as they move towards you and decrease in pitch as they move away?

7. What Node can be used to play a sound at a random pitch and volume each time it's played?

8. What is the scientific term for the reduction in strength of a signal?

9. What is the difference between the inner and outer Attenuation Shapes (by default a sphere) of an Ambient Sound Actor?

10. In order for Spatialization to work, does a sound need to be mono or stereo?

11. Name a free software application you can use to convert an audio file into a format that Unreal will accept.

Answers

1. .wav

2. Sound Cue

3. Ambient Sound Actor

4. The quality of that sound will increase at a cost of increasing the amount of memory required for the sound.

5. When you spawn a sound, you have control over it. You can choose to stop playing the sound at any point, or modify its properties. But when you play a sound, you don't have any control over it. You can't modify or stop it.

6. Doppler effect

7. Modulator Node

8. attenuation

9. At any point within the inner shape, the sound will be heard at 100% volume. In the outer shape, the sound will decrease in volume as it gets closer to the outer edge.

10. mono

11. Audacity

10

Additional Topics ⌄

10.1 Downloading Content From the Epic Games Launcher

This section will show you how to use the Epic Games Launcher to download content to use in the creation of your games. In the Epic Games Launcher, the *Learn* tab contains content you can download for free and the *Marketplace* tab contains content you can purchase.

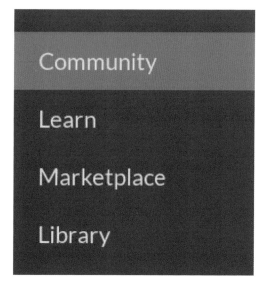

Figure 10.1.1 – The tabs of the Epic Games Launcher

Learn Tab

If you go to the Learn tab and scroll down, starting with the *Engine Feature Samples* category, you will find a lot of content you can use in your games and also sample projects that help to illustrate various concepts and features of the Engine.

For example, the *Open World Demo Collection* contains various meshes like grass, rocks, bushes and trees that you can use to make nice-looking outdoor terrains. There are downloads for water, mountains, particle effects, Blueprints, and so on. There's also projects you can download that demonstrate certain gameplay concepts or even entire sample games. You can click on any of the boxes to get more details and to actually download the content.

Figure 10.1.2 – Click on a box such as this one to learn more information about that content

Figure 10.1.3 – A sample platform game you can download for free from the Learn tab

Marketplace Tab

The Epic Games Marketplace is where you can find Assets to purchase. You can get to the Marketplace either by clicking on the Marketplace tab in the Epic Games Launcher, or by clicking on the Marketplace button in the Toolbar of the Level Editor.

The Marketplace is divided into various categories based on the Assets provided. For example, you have environments, materials, audio, and so on. You can get to the various categories either by scrolling through the page, or by using the links in the menu to go straight to the category. Same as the Learn tab, just click on the boxes to learn more about that content or to download it.

Vault

When you download something through the Learn tab or the Marketplace, you can access it by clicking on the *Library* tab and going down to the *Vault* section. If the content is a sample project, you can click on the yellow button under its name to create that project. If the content is a group of Assets, you can click on the yellow button to add those folders to the Content Browser of an existing project that you specify.

Figure 10.1.4 – Access content you download through the Vault section of the Library tab

10.2 Importing 3D Objects From the Internet

This section will show you a couple more places where you can find free 3D objects to download, and how to import those objects into Unreal Engine.

Tf3dm.com

One great website to get free 3D models from is *tf3dm.com*. You can use the search box to look for something specific, or you can browse the categories using the icons. Under the description of the category will be a row of subcategories you can browse to.

Figure 10.2.1 – The search box at tf3dm.com

Figure 10.2.2 – The different categories available are represented by these icons

One of the great things about this site is that it is specifically devoted to free 3D objects. There is a strip at the top advertising 3D models for a price, but other than that, all the results that appear will be free to download. However, something you need to be aware of that is very important if you're planning on making games that you charge money for, is that just because an Asset is free to download, that doesn't necessarily mean you are free to use it in a commercial game (a game that makes money).

For example, some Assets come with a *Personal Use Only* license. This means you're allowed to download it, and import it in your projects, and make a game with it; but the only thing you can do with that game is play it yourself or perhaps give it away for free to a few friends. If you started charging money for the game, the person who created the Asset would be allowed to sue you for violating the terms of the license.

So if you want to find objects that are free to use in commercial games, you can check the checkbox under the search bar labeled "Commercial license only" and then run the search again. This will filter the results down to only those with *Commercial Use* licenses. However, you still need to see if the Asset comes with any further stipulations. Often, the artist will require you to credit them in the work in order for the license to be valid.

Another great thing about this site is that it doesn't require you to have an account to download. So when you're ready to download an object, simply click on the blue Download button, and it will download a zip file containing the object in all the different file formats listed below the button. The only 3D object type that Unreal Engine can directly import is the *.fbx* file type.

Figure 10.2.3 – The download button will download a zip file containing the file formats listed in the box below the button

Luckily, most of the websites you can download 3D objects from have a way for you to narrow down the results to a specific type you're looking for. For example, on this site, there will be a strip of buttons showing the different file types available, and clicking on a type will narrow the results down to only objects that have a version of that type available. So if you click on "fbx" you will only see those objects that are available as an .fbx file.

| .3dm | .3ds | .blend | .c4d | .dae | .dwg | .dxf | .fbx | .lwo |

Figure 10.2.4 – You can filter your results by file format

Cgtrader.com

Another 3D-object website you can use is *cgtrader.com*. You can use the search bar, or if you want to browse by category, you can go up to the top of the page, hover over "3D models" and then click on the category you're interested in. From there, you can choose to either browse that category as a whole or click down into one of its subcategories.

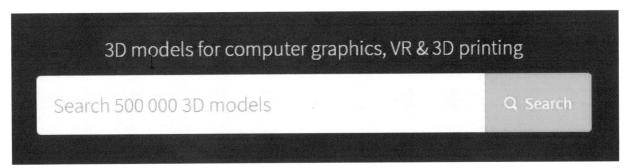

Figure 10.2.5 – The search box at cgtrader.com

Figure 10.2.6 – You can browse the various categories available by clicking on the 3D models menu at the top of the home page

By default, you will mainly see listings of the objects for sale, so if you're only interested in the free objects, you will need to check the "Free" checkbox. The first row will still contain premium content, but after that you will only see results for objects that can be downloaded for free. This site has a dropdown you can use to search by file type.

Figure 10.2.7 – Narrow results down by price and/or file format

Just like with the last site, or any site that you download artistic content from, make sure you check the details to see what kind of license agreement it has and what the terms of that agreement are. Unlike the last site, you will need to have an account in order to download from cgtrader.com.

Importing .fbx Files

Importing .fbx files into Unreal Engine works pretty much the same as importing any other file. You can either use the Import button in the Content Browser, or drag-and-drop the files into the Content Browser directly.

One difference when importing an .fbx file, however, is that the import is heavily customizable. A popup menu will appear giving you a long list of options regarding how you want the object imported.

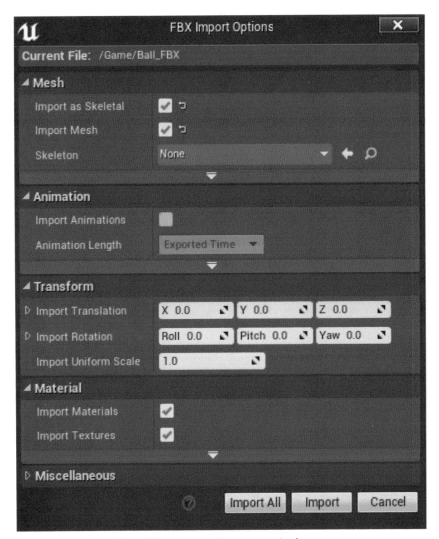

Figure 10.2.8 – The FBX Import Options window

For example, if the object is a static mesh, it will, by default, import it as a Static Mesh. But if you wanted to import it as a Skeletal Mesh, you could check the *Import as Skeletal* checkbox. You also have the option to have the importer automatically generate the object's collision properties.

By default, the object will be added to the center of the Level, with it rotated and scaled the same as it was when it was exported, but you can change these settings if you wish. You can also choose if you want the Materials and Textures imported as well, or if you only wish to import the underlying mesh. When all the options are to your liking, you simply need to click the Import button to complete the import. You may get some warning messages if the file wasn't formatted exactly how the Engine likes it, but often, the import will still work.

One thing you need to be aware of, however, is that, even with the restriction of only being able to import .fbx files, and despite Epic Games' best efforts, the system is still far from perfect. Most of the time, the mesh itself will import without any problem, but there are still considerable technical issues regarding Materials and Textures importing properly. Because of this, Epic Games actually recommends that all Materials be applied within the Unreal Editor itself, rather than trying to import them in already applied to the mesh.

10.3 Chapter 10 Quiz

1. What tab of the Epic Games Launcher contains content you can download for free?

2. What tab of the Epic Games Launcher contains content you can download for a price?

3. When you download something through the Learn or Marketplace tabs of the Epic Games Launcher, how do you access it?

4. True or False: If an Asset is made available to download for free by its owner, this means you can use it in your games without restriction.

5. What file format does a 3D model need to be in for Unreal to import it?

6. Is it better to apply a Material to a mesh before or after importing it into Unreal?

Answers

1. Learn tab

2. Marketplace tab

3. In the Vault section of the Library tab of the Epic Games Launcher.

4. False. You *might* be able to use it without restriction, but being available as a free download isn't an indication of this. You will need to check the licensing requirements that have been specified by the owner.

5. .fbx

6. It is better to apply a Material to a mesh *after* it has been imported into Unreal.

74785344R00188

Made in the USA
Columbia, SC
06 August 2017